Beautiful Cross Stitch
from Classic Quilt Designs

Beautiful
Cross Stitch
from
Classic Quilt Designs

BRENDA DAY

Photographs by Steve Tanner

Illustrations by Penny Brown

Sterling Publishing Co., Inc.   New York
A STERLING / MUSEUM QUILTS BOOK

Acknowledgments

My thanks are due to Susan Jenkins of Museum Quilts, for without her collection of quilts this book would not exist.

Also to Ljiljana Baird, my editor, who used every means at her disposal to see it to its culmination, and to all the staff at Museum Quilts for their kind help.

To my stitchers, Joan Winwood, Cindy Bishop, Joanne Szafran, Mary Skelding and Wendy Lee for their wonderful stitching, against the clock in many cases.

To Vivienne Wells, who painstakingly edited the charts and instructions, and to Penny Brown for her clear and concise technical illustrations.

Last but not least to my husband, Charles, who encouraged and listened patiently throughout it all.

A STERLING/MUSEUM QUILTS BOOK

Published by Sterling Publishing Company, Inc.,
387 Park Avenue South, New York, NY 10016
and by Museum Quilts Publications Inc.
Published in the UK by Museum Quilts (UK) Inc.,
254-258 Goswell Road, London EC1V 7EB
Distributed in Canada by Sterling Publishing
c/o Canadian Manda Group, One Atlantic Avenue, Suite 105
Toronto, Ontario, Canada M6K 3E7
Distributed in Australia by Capricorn Link (Australia) Pty Ltd.,
P.O. Box 6651, Baulkham Hills Business Centre
NSW 2153, Australia

Copyright © Museum Quilts Publications, Inc. 1996

Text & Charts © Brenda Day 1996
Illustrations © Penny Brown 1996
Photographs © Steve Tanner 1996

Editor: Ljiljana Ortolja-Baird
Designer: Roger Davies

A CIP catalogue record for this book is available from the British Library

ISBN: 0-8069-1342-8

Printed and bound by Oriental Press, Dubai

Contents

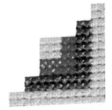

Introduction

On a pleasant morning in October 1983, my daughter and I arrived at the Guildhall Art Gallery in London. The flags were flying, but the place appeared to be deserted. Our suspicions were confirmed by the attendant at the door: the exhibition which we had traveled from North Wales to see was indeed closed. Our faces must have registered disappointment for, after instructing us to wait, the attendant disappeared, returning a few minutes later with a key. We were led down a corridor to the exhibition hall. The door was unlocked, the lights turned on and a veritable treasure house of color, pattern and texture revealed. So began my love affair with patchwork quilts, an interest which has grown over the years and developed into this book.

I have always been fascinated by the endless patterns devised by quilters, using just one basic block pattern. By simply changing the color of the fabric or the pattern or changing the orientation of a block, the quilter can create a completely different quilt. For me as a designer, this holds endless possibilities for creative exploration. A chance meeting with Susan Jenkins and her breathtaking collection of American quilts galvanized me into action. I was suddenly aware that with my next body of cross-stitch work I wanted to revisit the simple, geometric patterns originating from folk-art embroidery.

Cross stitch started off as a simple form of decorative needlework, favored by many folk traditions throughout the world. The geometric motifs, frequently repeating, were worked as borders on table and bed linen and as decoration on national costumes. The "squared-off" look created by the intersecting straight lines of the cross stitch naturally favored geometric designs, and if a cross stitcher decided to depict representational motifs such as people and animals, the image would have a primitive, angular appearance, a bit like a "Lego" construction.

Over the years, and certainly with Victorian needlewomen who had more time and more resources, cross stitch was coaxed into creating curves and circles to make intricate flower shapes and larger pictorial designs. The availability of a much extended range of colored embroidery threads due to the introduction of aniline dyes enabled cross stitchers to play with depth and illusion, thereby creating more sophisticated embroidery pictures.

During my two decades as a designer I have explored the many dimensions of cross-stitch embroidery, from the simple, one-color repeat motifs that can be stitched in an afternoon, to the intricate multi-colored picture designs, full of shading and 3-dimensional illusion, that can take several months to complete. I enjoy the challenges of both and am constantly on the lookout for new design inspirations.

From a vast selection of quilts I chose a number that would translate well into cross-stitch designs. The long line of repeating triangles in the nineteenth-century Flying Geese quilt would be ideal for the continuous border design on a bolster cushion. The thin, oblong shapes arranged around a small central square of the Log Cabin quilts offered many exciting design possibilities. Arranged in a light and dark sequence, this pattern was ideal for my design of a large-scale chessboard. The Amish Nine-patch quilt worked in small squares of glowing colors was my inspiration for the colorful footstool which I worked on black Aida to give added drama. The Schoolhouse pattern, a great favorite among quilters, translated wonderfully into a cross-stitch sampler.

Although I have concentrated on geometric designs drawn from "pieced" quilts, Susan Jenkins' collection also houses some outstanding appliqué quilts. The Ketcham Family Album quilt is a quilt of special beauty. The quilt has 36 blocks, each appliquéd with a different motif, some embroidered and some worked in delicate nineteenth-century chintz fabrics. The exquisite beauty was irresistible and I had to design a few items, in its memory. The Rose Picture was a real feat of color arrangement, for I was anxious to repeat in my cross-stitch picture the faded delicacy of old chintz.

Inspiration for cross-stitch designs can come from any number of different sources but I feel certain that all cross stitchers will agree with me after they have leafed through the pages of this book, when I say that quilts are truly a great source of inspiration. The quilts that I have chosen are but just a few of thousands of patterns that can be explored. Use my designs as a starting point; feel free to change the color scheme of a project, or the scale to highlight a different design element or to make the project fit in with your decor. Be adventurous! I have had a wonderful time exploring quilts and cross stitch. Good luck!

Charles Hadyn Day
×××××× Penley Madras School ××××××
September 1975-1977
¦¦¦¦¦ Llangollen Junior School ¦¦¦¦¦
September 1977-1979
×××××××× Dinas Brân School ××××××××
September 1979-1986

Charlotte Emma Day
×××××× Penley Madras School ××××××
September 1976-1977
¦¦¦¦¦ Llangollen Junior School ¦¦¦¦¦
September 1977-1980
×××××××× Dinas Brân School ××××××××
September 1980-1987

Schoolhouse Sampler Wallhanging

This sampler provides a permanent and decorative record of a child's school life. The original was worked for my son and daughter, but the design can be adapted for more or fewer children by increasing or reducing the number of motifs. Shown here as a wallhanging, the schoolhouse sampler would look just as effective as a framed picture.

SKILL LEVEL

Finished size (worked area):
14 x 12¼in
Stitch count: 172 x 197

MATERIALS

19 x 16¼in Zweigart driftwood/flecked-oatmeal 14-count Yorkshire Aida (3222/054)

14 x 16in red cotton fabric for backing, plus 2 strips 14 x 1¾in for triangular edging

13in wooden doweling, ⅜in diameter

2 small brass knobs with screw fittings for terminals

Small piece of cardboard, 2¼in wide, for tassel construction

Graph paper

Tissue paper

Machine thread

Tapestry needle 24

COATS ANCHOR STRANDED COTTON

(with number of skeins for embroidery and tassels)

⊞	46 x 4
⊞	01 x 2
⊞	401 x 2

⊞	8581 x 6
⊞	943 x 1

BACKSTITCH

401

STITCHES AND STRANDS

Cross stitch, using 2 strands of cotton

Backstitch (401), using 1 strand for windows, 2 strands for lettering and 2 strands for inner border

WORKING THE EMBROIDERY

1 Find the center of the Aida by folding into four. Find the center of the chart by counting squares. Start stitching at the center point and work the sampler following the chart. Leave the lettering until last.

2 Plan your lettering on a sheet of graph paper, allowing 1 square between the letters and numbers, and 4 squares between the words. Make sure that each line is centered, using the chart for positioning. The small patterns on some of the lines can be reduced or increased, depending on the amount of lettering.

3 When the stitching is complete, check for mistakes and loose ends, and press gently on the wrong side, onto a soft towel.

MAKING UP THE WALLHANGING

1 To make up as a wallhanging, place the two strips of red cotton fabric right sides together, and tack.

2 Trace the triangular border onto tissue paper. Place the tracing on the two strips, in the center, and tack along the zigzag line of the triangles. Tear away the tissue paper.

3 Machine or hand stitch along the zigzag tacking line. Remove the tacking stitches. Trim surplus fabric from around the points, leaving a strip of fabric ¼in around each point. (Do not trim the fabric along the bases of the triangles.) Clip the inner points and trim the outer ones (see diagram on page 14). Turn triangular strip inside out and press carefully into shape.

4 Tack and then machine stitch from end to end of the strip, along the bases of the triangles.

5 Place the triangular edging onto the front of the sampler, along the bottom edge, with the points pointing upward and the bases of the triangles two blocks of Aida below the last line of cross stitch. Tack securely along this line, then machine stitch.

6 Place sampler and red cotton backing right sides together and tack along the sides, four blocks of Aida outside the last line of cross stitch. Tack along the bottom. Machine stitch the sides, along the tacking lines, stopping 2¼in from the top to leave open the top edge. Machine stitch the bottom,

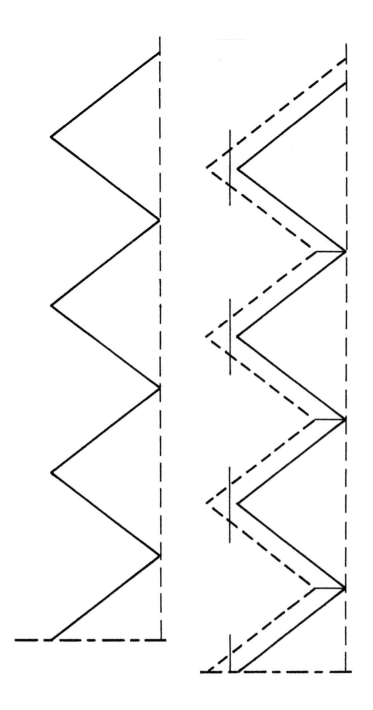

Half-pattern for Edging

Half-pattern for Edging
showing cutting line, clip
marks and trim lines.

abcdef ghijklmnopqrstuvwxyz
ABCDEFGHIJKLMNOPQRS
TUVWXYZ
1234567890

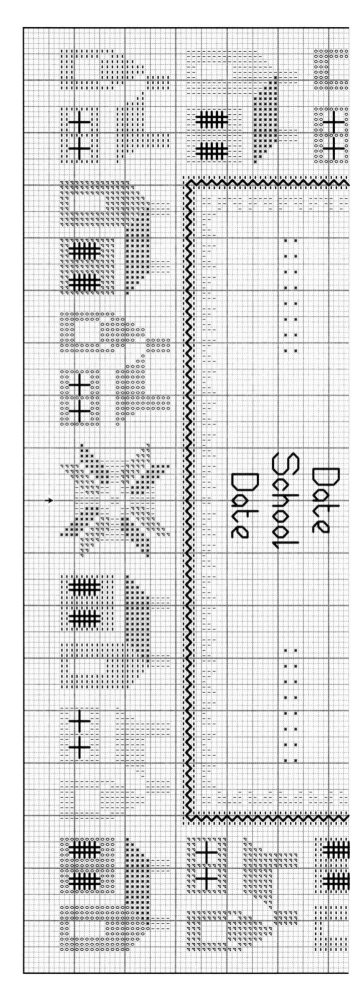

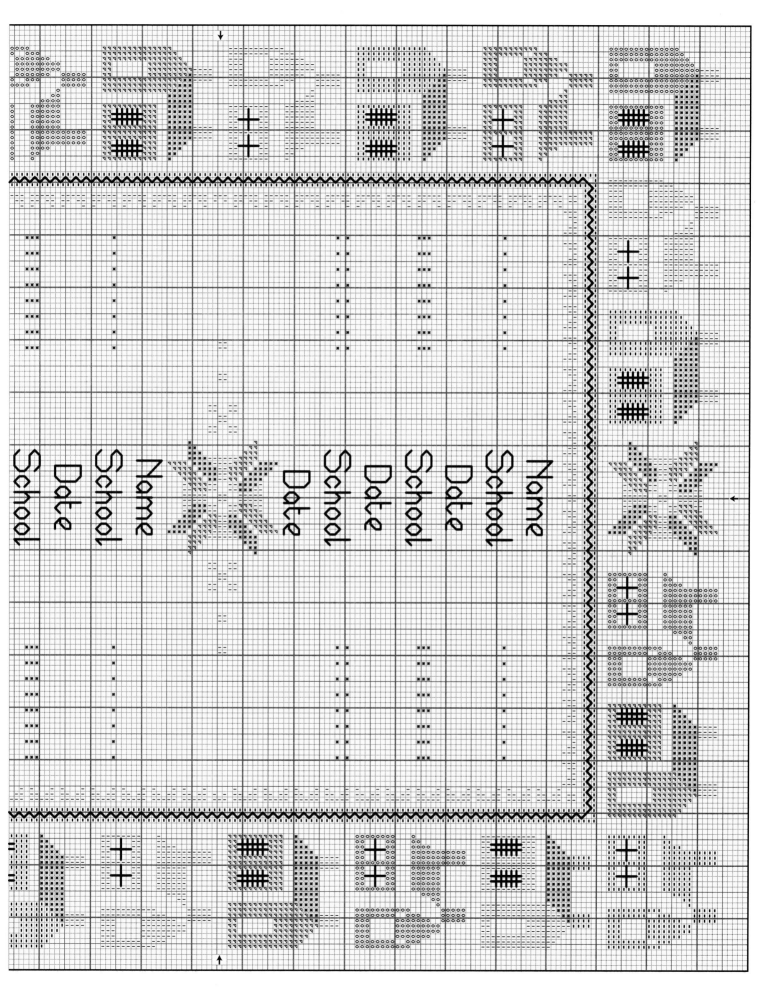

along the line of the previous machine stitching, joining front and edging.

7 Trim the bottom and side seams to ¼in from the machine line (see diagram).

8 Oversew along the side edges of the front of the sampler, where the side seams are open at the top. Turn the sampler right sides out and press carefully from the wrong side onto a soft towel.

9 Pin the front and back together at the top, and tack in a line, two blocks above the top line of cross stitches. Machine stitch along this line. Trim the backing fabric to ¼in from this line and oversew this edge of the backing fabric.

10 Turn the top of the sampler over onto the backing, turn the Aida under and slipstitch a neat hem along the line of machine stitching, forming a channel wide enough for the wooden doweling rod.

11 Make 6 small tassels (see page 126) using 2 skeins of Anchor 8581 and attach them to the bottom of the sampler, between the points of the edging. Make 2 tassels using 1 skein of Anchor 46 and attach them to the outer corners of the edging.

12 Insert the wooden doweling rod into the top channel and screw the brass knobs into the ends of the rod. Make a length of cord (length to fit hanging situation) using Anchor 8581 and attach it to the brass knobs, using a little Anchor 46 to bind in place as if finishing a tassel, and forming a loop large enough to slip over the knob.

Rainbow Schoolhouses
USA, c. 1940
76 x 80in
Museum Quilts Gallery, London

Schoolhouse and Stars Cushion

Based on the colorful 1940s quilt opposite, this project is worked on 11-count Aida, so it is ideal for complete beginners. It uses the schoolhouse motifs and several variations of the bright stars which adapt perfectly into clean, simple cross-stitch shapes. The cushion has a piped edge, which you could make yourself using a fine cord edging covered with fabric in your chosen color. Why not vary this design and make a set of cushions in different complementary colors — or ring the changes by altering the color of the piping?

SKILL LEVEL

Finished size: 16 x 16in
Stitch count: 117 x 117

MATERIALS

18 x 18in white Zweigart 11-count Aida

18 x 18in navy-blue glazed cotton

2yd blue piping

OR 2yd fine piping cord plus ½yd fabric in chosen color

16 x 16in cushion pad

Tapestry needle 22

COATS ANCHOR STRANDED COTTON

(1 skein of each)

⊞	128
◇◇	129
⊹⊹	131
▭▭	132
✳✳	134
∷	149
▪▪	323
⁄⁄	332
℘℘	1015

BACKSTITCH

127

323

STITCHES AND STRANDS

Cross stitch, using 3 strands of cotton

Backstitch, using 2 strands of cotton

WORKING THE EMBROIDERY

1 Find the center of the Aida fabric by folding into four. Find the center of the charted area by counting the squares. Mark the center of the fabric with a pin and the center of the chart with a pencil cross.

2 Start by stitching the inner border, counting out from the center. This will ensure that the design is centered and that the houses and stars are in the correct position. Work all the cross stitch before adding the backstitch details.

3 When the embroidery is completed, tack stitch a square measuring 16 x 16in around the outside of the worked area, making sure that the center point of this square matches exactly the center point of the worked area. This square marks the edges of the finished cushion and will act as a stitching guide.

4 Check for mistakes and loose threads, and press gently on the wrong side, onto a soft towel.

5 To make up the cushion and piping, follow the instructions given on pages 124-125.

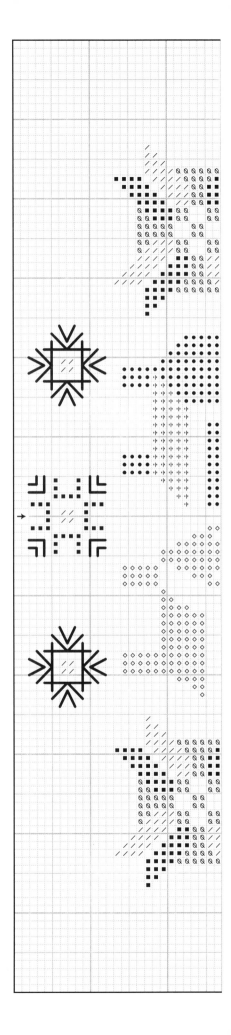

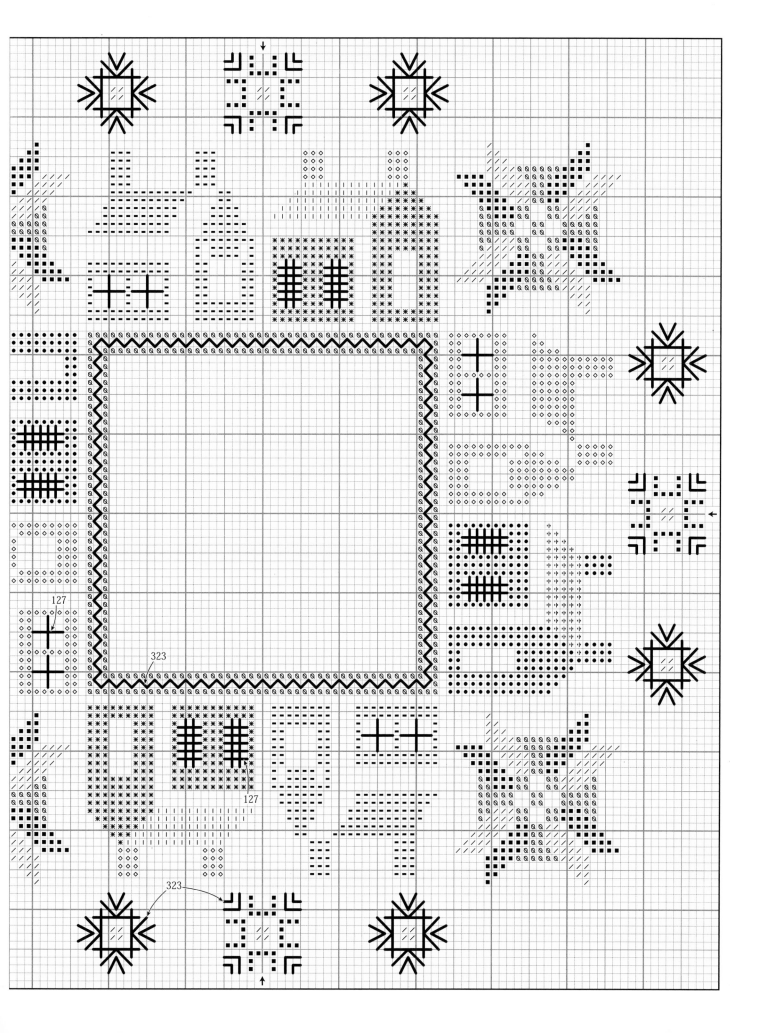

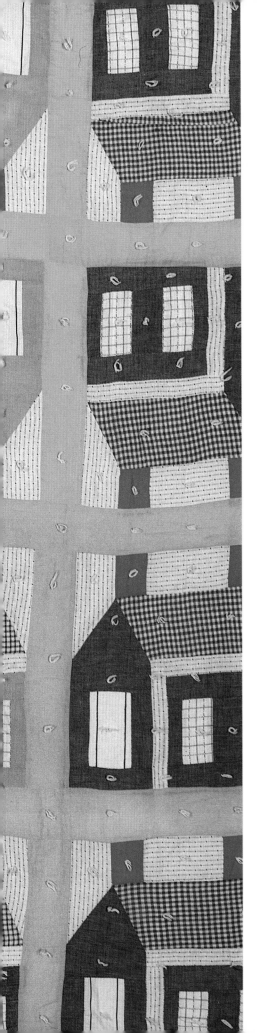

Schoolhouse Bell-Pull

In the unsettled and dangerous world of the new frontier, the one-room schoolhouse became a potent symbol of longed-for safety and security. Today the schoolhouse remains one of the most popular patterns among quiltmakers, and its simple geometric design makes it an ideal motif for cross stitch.

Echoing the homespun colors of the quilt, the unbleached linen and red edging of the Zweigart band provide the perfect fabric for this cross-stitch design.

The cross-stitch bell-pull records the dates when each of my children started school. You could stitch just the schoolhouse motifs first, then fill in the names and dates over the years, or you could make the bell-pull into a record of one child's school achievements. If you are planning your own version of the bell-pull, note the stitch count for each motif (house and lettering), count two threads of linen for each stitch, and remember to allow 2in at each end for hems.

Primitive Schoolhouses
Vermont, USA, c. 1880
60 x 70in
Museum Quilts Gallery, London

NOTE

Each square on the chart represents 2 x 2 threads of the fabric.

SKILL LEVEL

Finished size of bell-pull shown: 3¼ x 24in

Stitch count: each house, 22 x 22; house plus lettering below, 22 x 47

MATERIALS

28in Zweigart unbleached linen band, 3¼in wide, with red edging (7272/39)

Brass bell-pull fittings

Tapestry needle 24

COATS ANCHOR STRANDED COTTON

(1 skein of each)

⊞	01
⋰	46
и и	943
+ +	8581
⊠	401

BACKSTITCH

46

401

STITCHES AND STRANDS

Cross stitch, using 2 strands of cotton

Backstitch, using 1 strand (401) for windows, 2 strands (401) for lettering, and 2 strands (46) for stars

WORKING THE EMBROIDERY

1 Begin stitching the top house 3½in from the end of the band to allow enough fabric to make a hem for the top brass fitting. Make sure the house is centered, allowing 4 linen threads between the sides of the house and the innermost red edging.

2 Complete the cross stitch, following the chart. If names and dates are to be added over the years, leave spaces for this information, but work the red stars in between.

MAKING UP THE BELL-PULL

1 Measure 3½in from the bottom star and trim off any surplus.

2 Turn under ½in, then 1in at each end to make a hem, and stitch as invisibly as possible on the wrong side.

3 Attach the bell-pull fittings at each end. Press lightly on the wrong side onto a soft towel.

ABCDEFGHIJKLMNOPQRSTUVWXYZ
1234567890

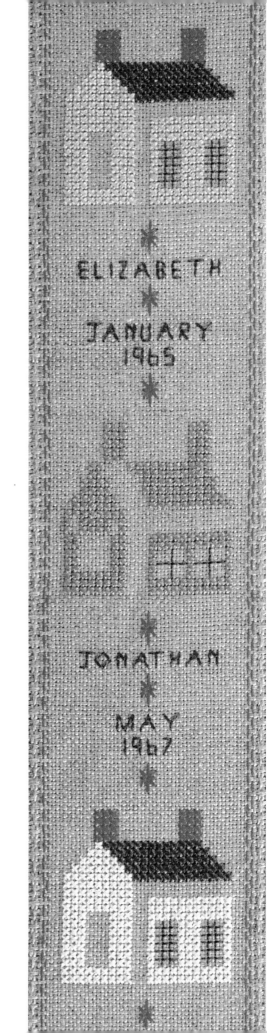

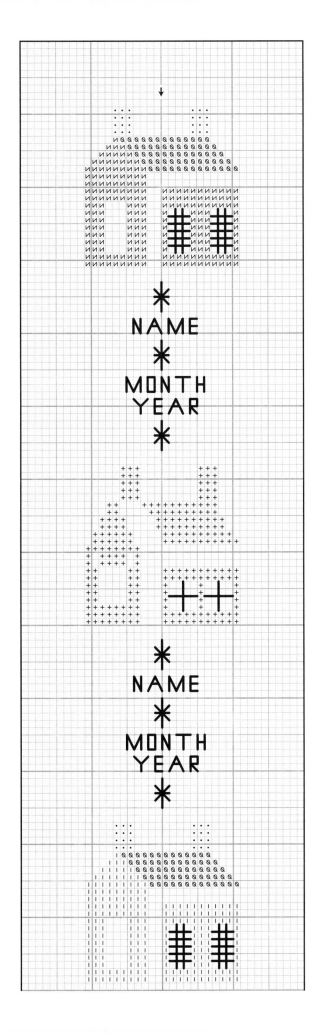

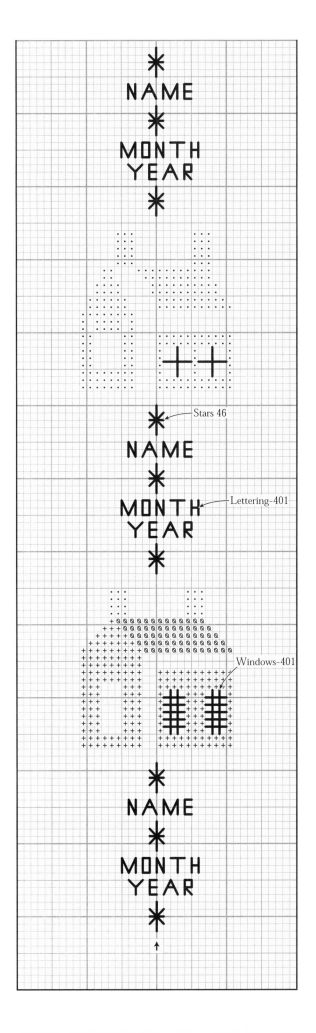

NAME

MONTH
YEAR

← Stars 46

NAME

MONTH
YEAR

← Lettering-401

← Windows-401

NAME

MONTH
YEAR

Tree of Life Cushion

This design is based on a blue-and-white Tree of Life quilt from the Blue Ridge Mountains in North Carolina, made around 1911. The quilt has been pieced with alternating diamonds of pastel blue and white, and the trees are made of coarse denim. I have reversed the colors to better recreate the strength of this design in cross stitch, using the diamond theme to make a centered panel for a cushion.

The random-dyed thread used for the leaves adds to the richness, and produces a cushion which is easy enough for a beginner to attempt, but very effective when worked. It is a good idea to cover the white cushion pad with navy-blue cotton so that the white does not show through the holes in the Aida. For this, you will need an extra quantity of cotton fabric (see over).

Tree of Life, North Carolina, USA, c. 1911, 62 x 74in, Museum Quilts Gallery, London

Finished size: 16 x 16in

Stitch count: 125 x 125

MATERIALS

18 x 18in navy-blue Zweigart 11-count Aida (589)

18 x 18in navy-blue glazed cotton for the cushion back (plus ½yd extra to cover cushion pad, if required)

2yd coordinating piping cord

16 x 16in cushion pad

Tapestry needle 22

COATS ANCHOR STRANDED COTTON

(with number of skeins)

⊞	1210 x 2
⊞	1211 x 2
⊟	146 x 1
⊡	143 x 1
⊞	177 x 1

STITCHES AND STRANDS

Cross stitch, using 3 strands of cotton

WORKING THE EMBROIDERY

1 Find the center of the Aida fabric by folding into four. Find the center of the charted area by counting the squares. Mark the center of the fabric with a pin and the center of the chart with a pencil cross.

2 Start by stitching the center square, and gradually work outward, following the chart and counting carefully.

3 When using the random-dyed thread, try not to create sudden jumps in color or tone. This can be avoided by matching the end of the thread which has just been used to the new length being started (it may be necessary to waste small amounts of thread in order to achieve this effect). Start stitching at one side of each tree, and work up and then down the vertical rows until the leaf area is completed.

4 When the embroidery is complete, tack stitch a square measuring 16 x 16in around the outside of the worked area, making sure that the center point of this square matches the center point of the worked area. This square marks the edges of the finished cushion and will act as a stitching guide.

5 Check for mistakes and loose threads, and press gently on the wrong side, onto a soft towel.

MAKING UP THE CUSHION

To make up the cushion, follow the instructions on page 124, or use the following very easy method.

1 With right sides together, tack front and back of the cushion together, leaving part of one side open in order to insert the pad.

2 Stitch along the tacked guide line, remove the tacking and turn right sides out.

3 Insert the cushion pad, and slip-stitch the opening.

4 Attach the piping cord around the edge using neat stitches, as invisibly as possible (see page 125).

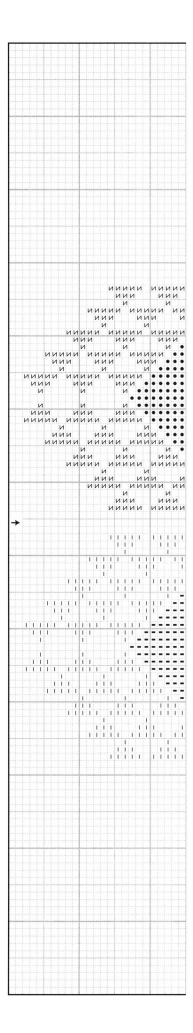

Nine-patch Footstool

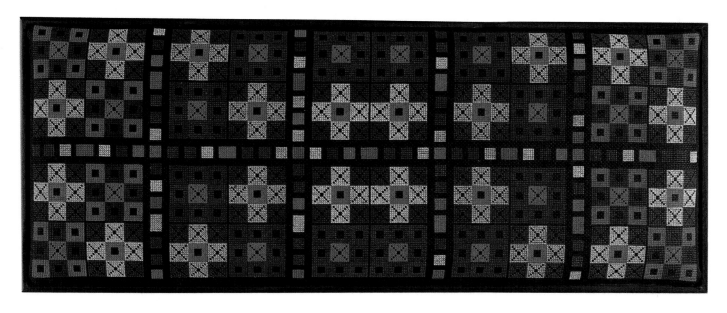

The glowing colors of the Amish Nine-patch quilt opposite, made around 1920 in Lancaster County, Pennsylvania, inspired this bold design for a stool top. The lines of small blocks between the large "nine-patch" squares refer back to the random collection of fabrics from which the quilter organized her quilt into a masterful design. This design can easily be rearranged to fit most sizes and shapes of stool. As this is a large piece of stitching, you will find it helps to use a slate or roller frame, starting at one end and rolling up the work as it is stitched.

Note that the chart shows one quarter of the whole design, and the diagram shows the layout for the complete design. The black outlined squares on the chart show the position of the small blocks of color.

SKILL LEVEL

Finished size of stool shown (recess):
27 x 10in

Size of worked area:
28 x 10½in

Stitch count: 138 x 363

MATERIALS

½yd black Zweigart 14-count Aida (3706/095/43)

½yd black fine cotton lining

Footstool Market Square
27 x 10in

Tapestry needle 24

Heavy-duty double-sided and single-sided adhesive tape (optional)

Upholstery tacks or heavy-duty staples
Dressmaker's pins (optional)

COATS ANCHOR STRANDED COTTON

⊞	246 x 1
⊠⊠	170 x 3
⊞	43 x 2
✳✳	19 x 1
⊞	123 x 2
⊞	204 x 1
⊘⊘	44 x 1
＞＞	832 x 2
◺	102 x 3
Ƨ Ƨ	148 x 3
▶▶	47 x 2
⊪	895 x 2

Amish Nine-patch, Pennsylvania, USA, c. 1920, 81 x 82in, Museum Quilts Gallery, London

STITCHES AND STRANDS

Cross stitch, using 2 strands of cotton

WORKING THE EMBROIDERY

1 Find the center of the Aida fabric by folding it in four. Find the center of the charted area by counting the squares. Mark the center of the fabric with a pin and the center of the chart with a pencil cross.

2 Start stitching from the center and complete the horizontal row of blocks, following the chart, which shows a random arrangement of colors.

3 Next, work the vertical rows which bisect the central row. You will now be able to position the squares of "nine-patch" blocks correctly. Note that the ends of the rows of small blocks are not intended to line up with the

squares; follow the chart carefully at this stage.

4 When the cross stitch is complete, check for mistakes, remove from the frame and press lightly on the wrong side onto a soft towel.

MAKING UP THE STOOL

1 Cover the upholstered pad of the stool with the fine black cotton, to

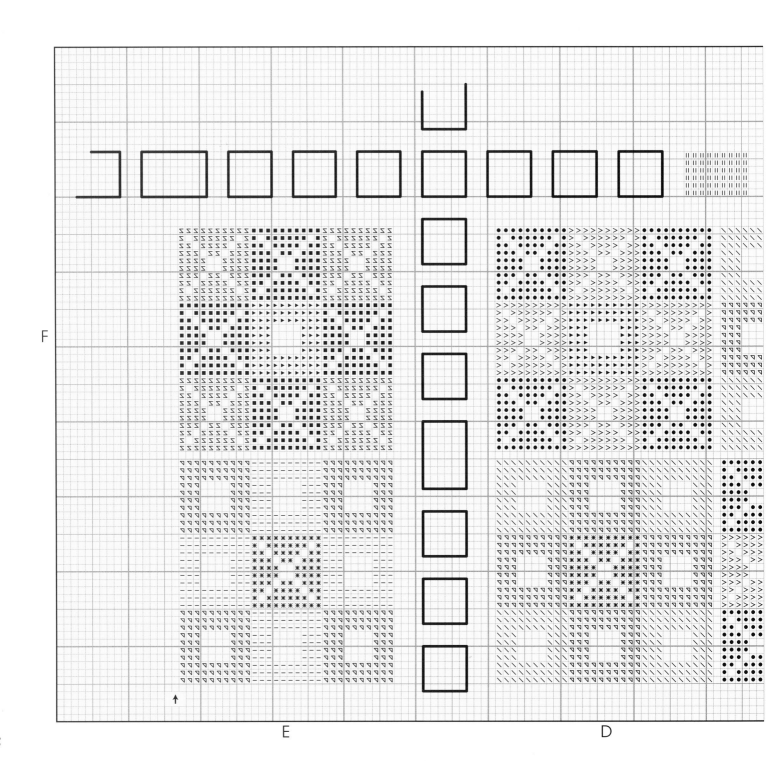

avoid the white covering fabric showing through the black Aida. Pleat any excess fabric at the corners. Secure with double-sided tape or upholstery tacks. Cut away any excess fabric.

2 Place the embroidery face down on a flat surface. Put the covered stool pad face down on top of the embroidery, lining up the centers of both pieces of fabric. It is helpful to place dressmaker's pins through the Aida into the pad as you position it. Treat the corners as before, but use upholstery tacks or heavy-duty staples to secure the Aida to the back of the pad. Cut away any surplus. If preferred, finish off the edges by securing them with double-sided adhesive tape.

3 Remove any dressmaker's pins and place the covered pad into the stool.

A	B	C	D	E	E	D	C	B	A
B	A	D	C	F	F	C	D	A	B

B	A	D	C	F	F	C	D	A	B
A	B	C	D	E	E	D	C	B	A

Cross-stitch layout

C   B   A

33

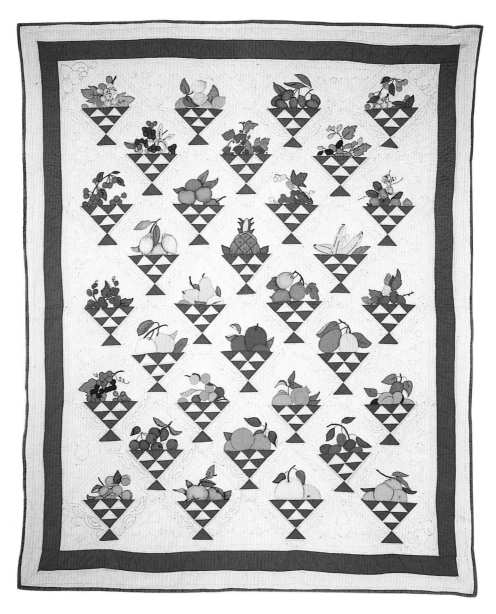

Baskets of Fruit, USA, c. 1930, 86 x 72in, Museum Quilts Gallery, London

Art Deco Fruit Baskets
Shelf Edging

The basket motif is a popular feature of many folk-art traditions and has been much used by generations of quilters. The simple, stylized baskets of this colorful Art Deco quilt adapt well into crisp cross-stitch shapes, contrasting pleasantly with the subtle shading and soft lines of the fruit.

Incorporated into a decorative shelf edging, this design brings a lively, folksy look to any kitchen or dresser. Measure your shelf to find out the final length of band required, then use the stitch count below to calculate how many baskets will be needed to fill the band. The quantities of stranded cotton required will depend on the size of your shelf.

For more ideas on using this versatile design, or parts of it, see the placemat and napkin featured on page 40.

SKILL LEVEL

Size: 5¼in wide x length to fit chosen shelf

Stitch count (each motif): 41 wide x 56 high (max)

MATERIALS

White Zweigart 16-count Aida band, 5¼in wide, with one damask edge (7229/1), length to fit chosen shelf

Tapestry needle 26

COATS ANCHOR STRANDED COTTON

(1 skein of each)

1007		842
11		844
45		846
210		292
875		278
879		852
893		851
1025		860
1027		854
403		859
313		1001
314		330

BACKSTITCH   403

STITCHES AND STRANDS

Cross stitch, using 2 strands of cotton

Backstitch, using 1 strand of cotton

WORKING THE EMBROIDERY

1 Cut your length of band to fit the chosen shelf, allowing a narrow hem at each end. Using the stitch count, calculate how many motifs are needed to fill the length, allowing 10 blocks between each basket. If necessary, adjust the amount of space left at each end, to give a balanced final design.

2 Begin stitching the first basket base about 2½in from the right-hand end of the band, on the third row of blocks from the bottom, following the chart. Complete the cross stitch for the whole motif, basket and fruit, before starting the backstitch.

3 When moving to the second basket, allow 10 blocks of space, and remember

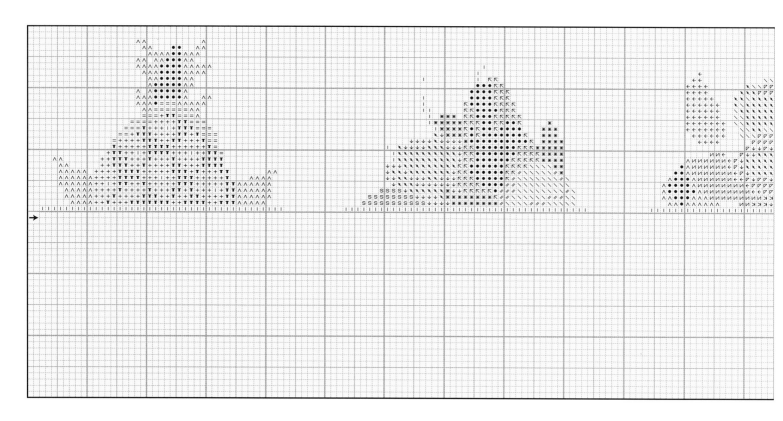

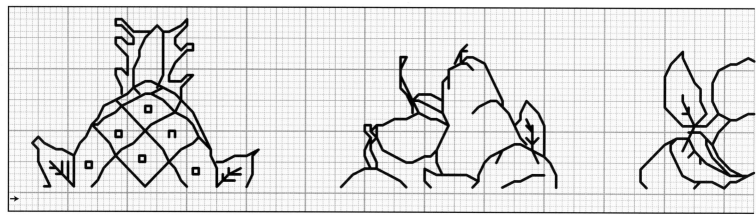

to leave the same number of blocks between all adjacent baskets.

4 When the stitching is finished, check for mistakes and loose ends. If required, press on the wrong side onto a soft towel.

5 Attach the edging to the shelf by pinning through the loops along the top edge. Alternatively, attach a strip

of plain white cotton fabric, the same length as the band, to the top edge of the band (before hemming the edges of the band). Hem the three raw edges. Pin through the plain fabric to fix the edging to the shelf.

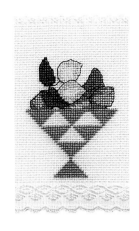

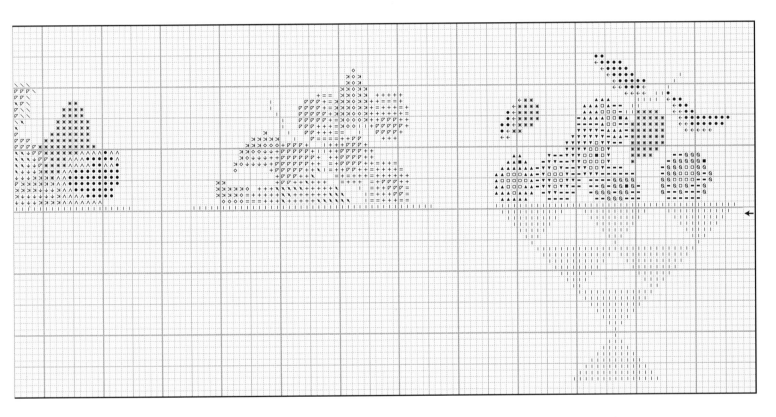

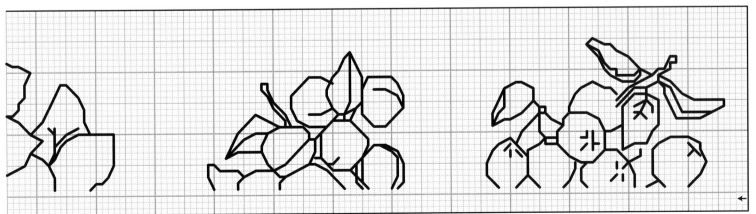

Art Deco Fruit Baskets
Placemat and Napkin

This pretty set of matching placemat and napkin owes its design to the same Art Deco quilt as the shelf edging, and features its own simple edging made of four-sided stitch and a fringe.

SKILL LEVEL

Finished size of placemat: 13¼ x 17in (excluding fringe)

Finished size of napkin: 11¾ x 11¾in (excluding fringe)

Stitch count (four-sided stitch): placemat, 93 wide x 116 high; napkin, 82 x 82

MATERIALS

14½ x 18in white Zweigart 14-count Aida for placemat

12¾ x 12¾in white Zweigart 14-count Aida for napkin

Tapestry needle 24

COATS ANCHOR STRANDED COTTON

(1 skein of each)

01 (four-sided stitch)

▥	1007
▤	11
▼▼	45
ss	210
▨	875
✱✱	879
◎◎	893
◇◇	1025
∧∧	1027
▦	403

BACKSTITCH

403

STITCHES AND STRANDS

Cross stitch, using 2 strands of cotton

Backstitch, using 1 strand of cotton

Four-sided stitch, using 2 strands of cotton worked over 4 blocks of fabric

WORKING THE EMBROIDERY

1 Work the placemat and napkin in the same way, starting with the four-sided stitch from the bottom right-hand corner, 7 blocks in from the bottom and right side (see page 121 for instructions on four-sided stitch). Refer to the stitch counts to make sure you stitch exactly the right number of four-sided stitches on all sides, otherwise the motifs will not fit as shown inside the edging. Note that the chart does not show the fabric outside the four-sided stitch.

2 Trim surplus fabric on top and left-hand edges, 6 blocks from the outside of the four-sided stitch.

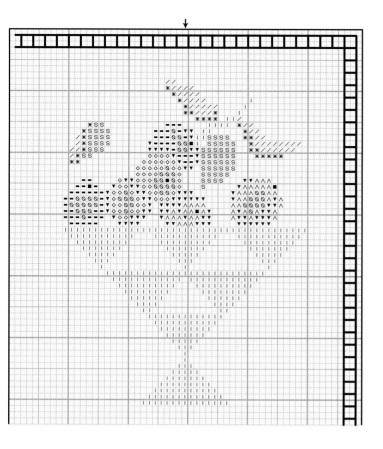

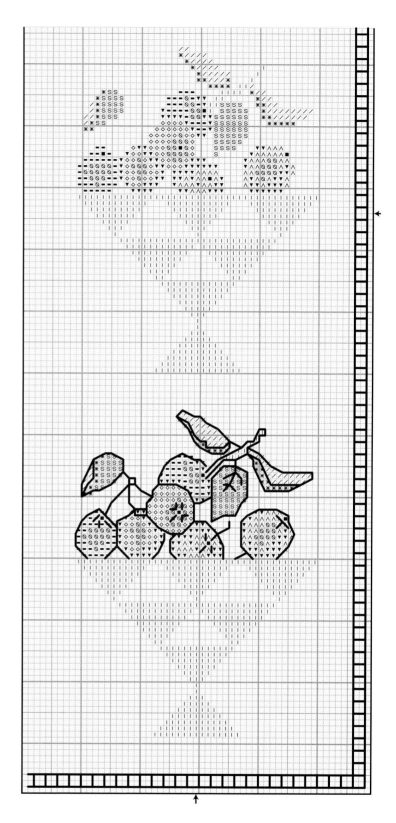

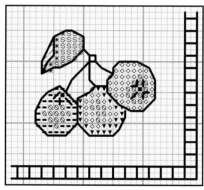

3 Begin the cross stitch, following the above charts for positioning the motifs in relation to the four-sided stitch. Follow the charts for stitching the basket of fruit motif.

4 Make the fringe by carefully pulling away the threads of the fabric outside the four-sided stitch, starting from a corner. Press on the wrong side, onto a soft towel.

Flying Geese, USA, c. 1880, 76 x 88in, Museum Quilts Gallery, London

Flying Geese Bolster Cushion

The strong vertical lines of the flying geese triangles in the 1880 Kentucky quilt opposite suggested a cross-stitch border on an elegant bolster cushion — great for a bed if you do not have a chaise longue! I have varied the size of the triangles to give more interest, used small patterns in the background to simulate the tiny prints from the original madder-style fabrics, and worked the center section of squares in soft grays to suggest the quilted background.

The cushion is finished with fat tassels attached to the centers of the end panels.

Note that the chart shows one half of the repeat design.

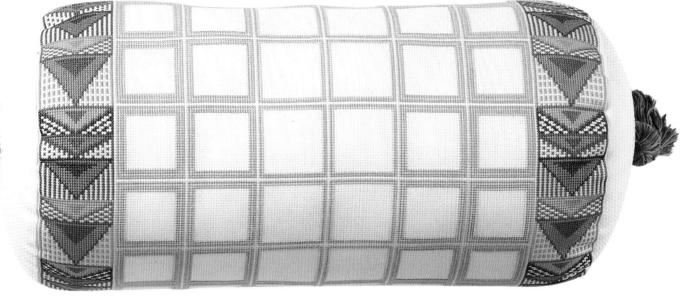

SKILL LEVEL

Finished size: 18in long by 8in in diameter

Stitch count: End motif 44 x 44 and main area 237 x 348

MATERIALS

21 x 30in white Zweigart 14-count Aida

Two 10in squares white Zweigart 14-count Aida

18 x 8in bolster cushion pad

Two 10in squares tissue paper

Tapestry needle 24

2 polystyrene balls, 1in diameter for the tassels

Strip of cardboard, 4½in wide

COATS ANCHOR STRANDED COTTON

(with number of skeins, inc tassels)

⬚	231 x 4	⬚	361 x 1
⬚	397 x 4	⬚	375 x 3
⬚	848 x 2	⬚	373 x 2
⬚	847 x 1	⬚	845 x 3
⬚	379 x 2	⬚	843 x 2
⬚	376 x 2	⬚	393 x 3
⬚	363 x 3	⬚	392 x 2

STITCHES AND STRANDS

Cross stitch, using 2 strands of cotton

WORKING THE EMBROIDERY

1 Take the large piece of Aida. Find the center of the shortest side. Match this to the right-hand edge of the right-hand square on the charted design. Start stitching 1½in up from the edge, in the center of the fabric, and stitch the three large squares, working from right to left.

2 Stitch a mirror image of the three squares, to the right of the center where you started, reversing the order of the squares.

3 Work the beginning of the triangle border at both ends of the row of squares.

4 Stitch 11 further rows of squares, leaving one row of Aida blocks between each row (see chart). There should be 12 rows of squares in total.

5 Continue stitching the borders, which repeat 5 times. Finish the borders by adding the second triangle to the end of the border, omitting its last line. The borders should now be one block longer than the section with the rows of squares.

6 Find the center point of one of the 10in squares of Aida, match this to the center of the chart of the square design for the ends of the cushion. Stitch, following the chart. Repeat with the other square for the other end of the cushion.

TO MAKE UP THE CUSHION

1 To make up the cushion, draw an 8in diameter circle on each square of tissue paper. Match their centers with the centers of the end panels. Pin in place and tack with small stitches along the pencil line. (This gives greater accuracy when making up, and thus a better shape.) Tear away the tissue paper. Trim the fabric to within ½in of the tacked circle.

2 Trim the large piece to within ½in of the embroidery. Fold in half, right sides together, matching the short sides so that the border pattern continues without a break. Tack the short sides together, then stitch, leaving a gap of approximately 8in in the center.

3 Set the circular end panels into the ends of the cushion, right sides together, using the tacked circles as a guide, and leaving one row of Aida blocks between the borders on the main panel and the seam line. Stitch carefully, easing in any fullness. Remove tacking threads. Turn right side out, and attach tassels to the ends if required (see below), stitching securely in place.

4 Insert cushion pad and slipstitch the opening.

TO MAKE THE TASSELS

1 Take 1 skein each of Coats Anchor Stranded Cotton in the following colors: 392, 379, 843, 373, 375, 363, 393 and 845. Use all of the thread to make two fat tassels, less to make smaller tassels.

2 Wind half of all the skeins around the width of the cardboard. (For ease of working, attach the ends to the cardboard with tape.) Anchor all the ends with more masking tape.

3 Run a matching thread under the wound threads at one edge of the cardboard. Pull up tightly and tie with a secure knot.

4 At the other edge of the cardboard, carefully cut the wound threads. Remove the cardboard.

5 Put a pin through the bound threads, where the matching thread is knotted, into one of the polystyrene balls. Arrange the threads evenly around the ball to cover it completely.

6 Using matching thread, bind the threads under the ball as tightly, and as close to the ball, as possible. Tie off tightly and arrange the ends of the binding thread in among the tassel threads so they are not visible.

7 Trim the bottom of the tassel neatly so that the threads are all the same length.

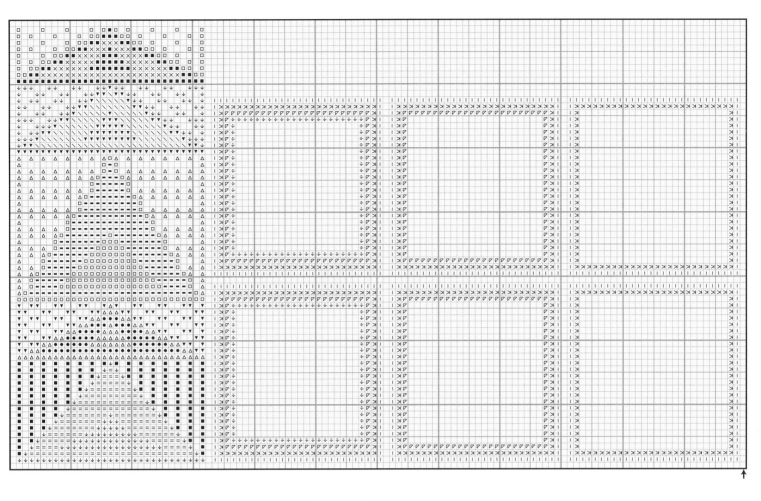

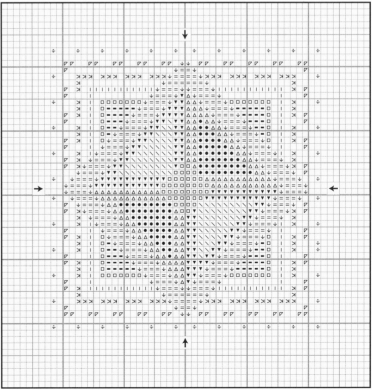

End Motif

Flying Geese Glasses Case

Though this project is based on the same quilt as the bolster cushion on page 45, I have used a richer color scheme in red, blue, and green. The back and front of the case use these colors slightly differently, though the design is exactly the same. If preferred, you could use just one of the charts for both front and back.

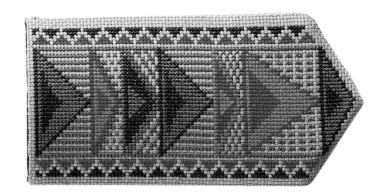

SKILL LEVEL

Finished size : 4 x 7½in

Stitch count : 43 x 95

MATERIALS

Two pieces 6 x 9in summer-khaki/olive Zweigart 14-count Aida (323)

Two pieces 6 x 9in lining fabric to match one of the stranded cotton colors

Two pieces 4 x 7½in Thermo-fuse

Matching sewing cotton

Tapestry needle 24

COATS ANCHOR STRANDED COTTON

(1 skein of each)

⊞	856
◹	921
▼▼	1036
◌◌	338
●●	1014

STITCHES AND STRANDS

Cross stitch, using 2 strands of cotton

WORKING THE EMBROIDERY

1 Find the center of the Aida fabric by folding into four. Find the center of the charted area by counting the squares. Mark the center of the fabric with a pin and the center of the chart with a pencil cross.

2 Start stitching from the center, following the chart.

3 When the two panels are completed, check for mistakes and loose threads, and press gently on the wrong side, onto a soft towel.

MAKING UP THE CASE

1 Place front and back panels right sides together. Stitch side and bottom seams, ¼in outside the embroidery. Leave the top open. Trim the seams, but not the top.

2 Turn the case right side out and press carefully under a cloth.

3 Cut the two pieces of stiffening ⅛in smaller than the stitched glasses case. Peel the paper backing from one side and attach the stiffening to the wrong sides of the pieces of lining fabric, parallel with the grain.

4 Place the two lining pieces right sides together and stitch the side and bottom seams ⅛in outside the stiffening. Leave the top open. Do not turn right sides out. Trim the stitched seams.

5 Turn over the top edges of the lining section and trim to ⅜in. Turn in the top edges of the Aida case, trimming if neccesary to match the lining.

6 Insert the lining into the Aida case and stitch together around the top, using slipstitch or ladder stitch.

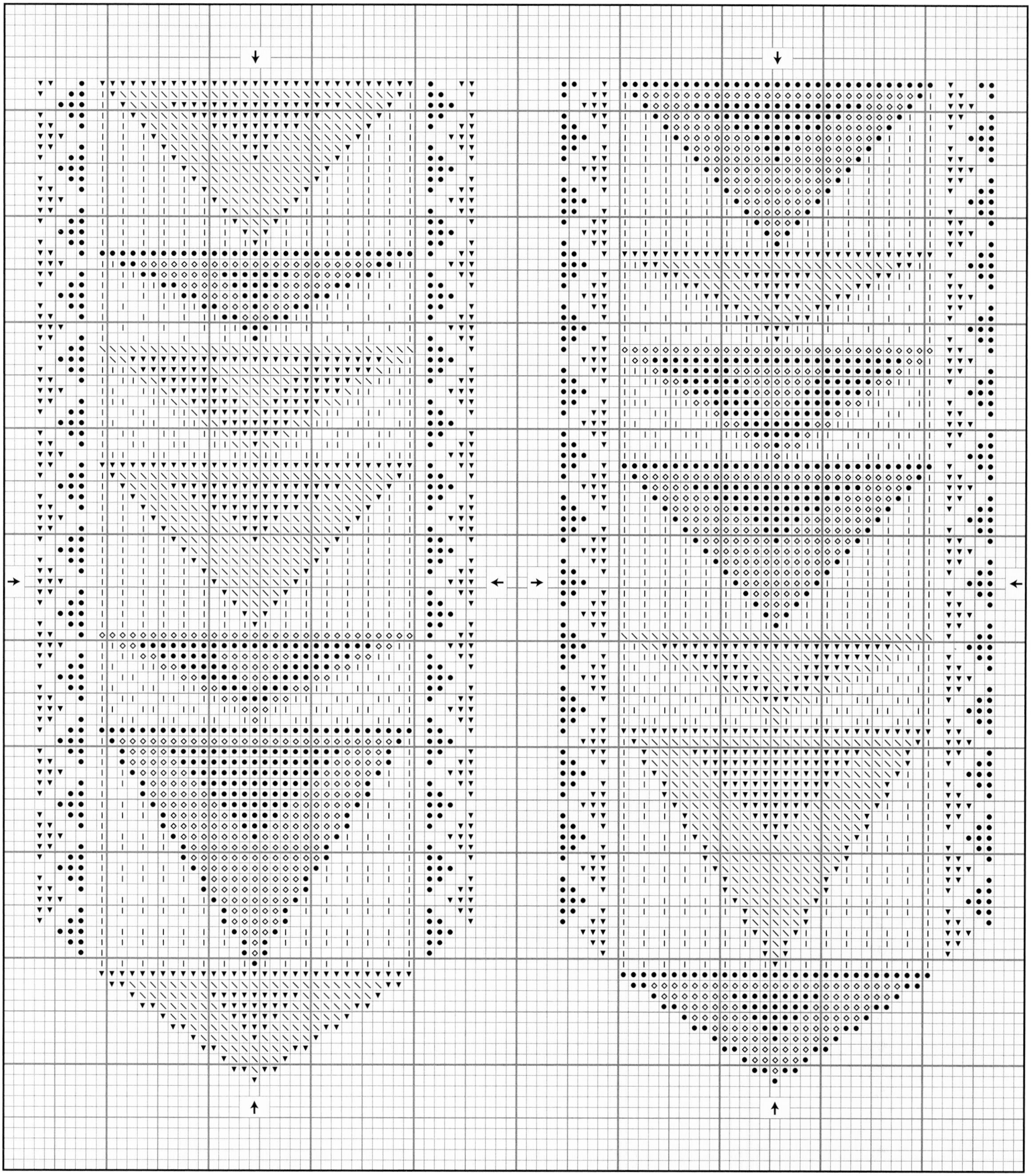

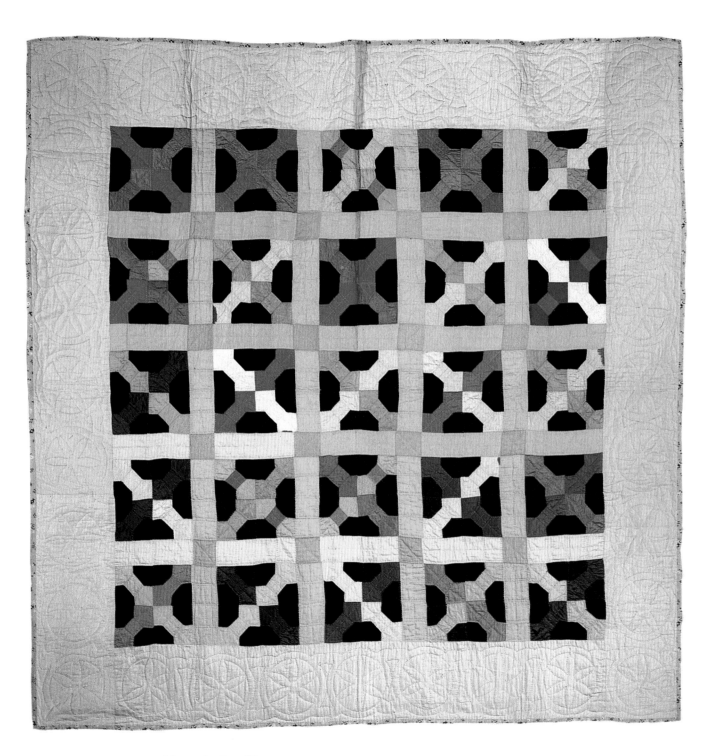

Mennonite Bow Tie, Ohio, USA, c. 1920, 75 x 75in, Museum Quilts Gallery, London

Bow-tie Cushion

This design is based on a 1920 Mennonite bow-tie quilt, composed of strongly colored squares set off by a pale pink border and dramatic broken black hexagons. The pink strips and pale gray squares dividing the central area of the quilt have been translated into satin ribbon and silver kid leather for this cross-stitch cushion. The whole effect is one of colorful opulence.

The narrow ribbon is couched down, and is attached by stitching over it, using matching cotton. It is recommended that you use a slate or roller frame for stitching this project.

Finished size of stitched area: 12 x 18⅞in

Finished cushion: 16 x 23¾in

Stitch count : 256 x 168

MATERIALS

19 x 26in oyster-pink / bisque Zweigart 14-count Aida (302)

19 x 26in backing fabric in a coordinating color

2 x 2in silver kid leather

16 x 24in cushion pad

Pale gray machine thread

Tapestry needle 24

Sharps or crewel needle 10

COATS ANCHOR STRANDED COTTON

(inc number of skeins)

⠿	400 x 6	
▥	893 x 1	
◔◔	895 x 3	
⬤⬤	74 x 2	
▿▿	68 x 2	
◉◉	43 x 2	
▰▰	234 x 3	
▽▽	323 x 2	
▪▪	326 x 2	
✳✳	47 x 2	
↑↑	46 x 2	

9 x 1 (only for couching the ribbon)

895 x 1 (only for couching the ribbon)

1012 x 1 (only for couching the ribbon)

868 x 1 (only for couching the ribbon)

OFFRAY DOUBLE-FACED SATIN RIBBON

1½yd light coral 238, ⅛in wide

1¾yd coral ice 205, ⅛in wide

1yd nude 112, ⅛in wide

3½yd sweet nectar 161, ⅛in wide

2yd nude 112, ⅜in wide

STITCHES AND STRANDS

Cross stitch, using 2 strands of cotton

Straight stitch for couching the narrow ribbon, using 2 strands of cotton and attaching the wide ribbon, using 1 strand of cotton

WORKING THE EMBROIDERY

1 Find the center of the Aida fabric by folding into four. Tack a central line in both directions, dividing the fabric into four. Attach the Aida to your stitching frame, following the instructions on page 117, and tensioning the fabric carefully.

2 Find the center of the chart by counting squares and mark with a pencil cross. Start stitching from the center and work all of the cross stitch before applying any ribbon.

3 When the embroidery is complete, cut the narrow ribbon into the following lengths.

Light coral (238): two lengths of 11in; two lengths of 7in; two lengths of 4in

Coral ice (205): two lengths of 11in; four lengths of 7in; two lengths of 4in

Nude (112): two lengths of 7in

Sweet nectar (161): four lengths of 7in; two lengths of 4in

4 Attach the ribbon lengths in the spaces between the embroidered blocks, placing each length one Aida block away from the embroidery. You will find it easier to apply first the 11in lengths, which run from the center to the ends of the cushion. Use a straight stitch to couch down the ribbon, the stitches being spaced every two Aida blocks.

5 Add the shorter lengths in the appropriate places, consulting the color illustration for positioning. Butt the short lengths of ribbon up to the

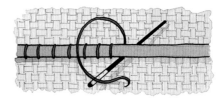

longer lengths. Do not turn the ends under. (The ends will project beyond the embroidery, and should be stitched for two blocks beyond the end of the cross-stitch areas.)

6 When all the cut ribbon is in place, starting at one corner, apply the nude ribbon, spacing it one block away from the embroidery. Stitch the inner edge down first with small, neat stitches, using one strand of matching cotton. Miter the corners, by folding the ribbon, as you come to them, and finally turn under the end of the ribbon on the last corner, making a neat, matching miter. Stitch the outer edge in the same direction, trimming off any surplus narrow ribbon which projects as you come to it.

7 Cut eleven ¼in squares from the silver kid leather. Apply one to each of the intersections of the narrow ribbon within the stitched area, catching down with small even stitches using machine thread.

8 Cut four ½in squares of silver kid leather and position with one corner three blocks diagonally outside the outer corner of the wide ribbon. Stitch in place as before.

9 Starting at one corner, stitch the remaining sweet nectar ribbon in place, one block outside the wide ribbon. Fold the ribbon around the silver kid squares, as you turn the corners. Finish the end off neatly when you reach the last corner.

10 To make up the cushion, follow the instructions given on page 124.

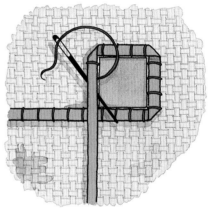

Bow-tie
Curtain Tieback

This colorful tieback originates from the same bow-tie quilt as the bow-tie cushion, and uses the same variety of materials to produce a very rich effect. Quantities are given for one tieback.

SKILL LEVEL

Finished size: 30½ x 3in

Stitch count : 418 x 40

MATERIALS

7 x 36in oyster-pink/bisque Zweigart 14-count Aida (302)

7 x 36in backing fabric in a coordinating color

4½ x 32in Pelform stiffening

3½ x 4½in silver kid leather

Pale gray machine thread

Tapestry needle 24

Sharps or crewel needle 10

2 small brass rings

COATS ANCHOR STRANDED COTTON

(with number of skeins)

⬚	400 x 2	
⬚	893 x 1	
⬚	895 x 2	to include couching ribbon
⬚	74 x 2	to include couching ribbon
⬚	68 x 1	
⬚	43 x 1	
⬚	323 x 1	
⬚	326 x 1	
⬚	47 x 1	
⬚	46 x 1	
	9 x 1	(only for couching the ribbon)
	1012 x 1	(only for couching the ribbon)

OFFRAY DOUBLE-FACED SATIN RIBBON

1yd nude 112, ⅛in wide

1yd pink 150, ⅛in wide

1yd sweet nectar 161, ⅛in wide

1yd light coral 238, ⅛in wide

2yd sweet nectar 161, ⅝in wide

STITCHES AND STRANDS

Cross stitch, using 2 strands of cotton
Straight stitch for couching the narrow ribbon, using 2 strands of cotton

For attaching the wide ribbon, use 1 strand of cotton

WORKING THE EMBROIDERY

1 Fold the Aida strip in half down its length, and start by stitching the triangle,

placing it centrally on the fold, and positioning the point 2in from the end of the fabric.

2 Work the four squares shown in the chart, then repeat them. Then repeat the first square again. Always leave the same amount of space between the squares, as shown on the chart. Finish by working another triangle to match the first. Work all the cross stitch before applying the ribbons.

MAKING UP THE TIEBACK

1 Cut the narrow ribbon into 4in lengths. Space two strips evenly between the embroidered units, mixing the colors. The ribbon should project ½in beyond the edge of the embroidery on both sides. Stitch in place with straight stitches every two blocks, using two strands of matching cotton.

2 Cut the wide ribbon into two 36in lengths. Position the ribbon along each side of the embroidered strip, overlapping the fine ribbons, and leaving two blocks between the embroidery and the broad ribbon. Stitch the inside edge first. Trim the ends level with the first row of the triangular end units. Stitch the outer edge of the ribbon, working in the same direction, and finally catch the ends with a few stitches. The stitching should be as invisible as possible.

3 Cut twenty ¾in squares of silver kid leather. Place one square over each ribbon intersection, lining up with the inner edge of the wide ribbon. Stitch in place carefully.

4 Check for mistakes and loose ends. Press on the wrong side, if necessary, onto a soft towel.

5 Cut the Thermo fuse to measure 31⅜ x 4½in and miter the ends, matching the angle of the cross-stitch triangles.

6 Lay the embroidery face down on a clean surface. Place the stiffening on top, positioning the end point of the stiffening ½in beyond the embroidered point. Peel off a small amount of the underside backing paper, position the point and beginning of the strip, using the extreme outer edge of the stitched kid squares as a guide. Carry on peeling off the backing and positioning a little at a time until the other end is reached. Press into place carefully. Trim the surplus fabric to ½in.

7 Remove the backing from the top side of the Pelform, and turn the surplus fabric onto the adhesive surface, mitering the corners where necessary.

8 Place the lining fabric face down, and put the stiffened tieback centrally on top of the lining. Press into place. Trim the surplus fabric to ½in. Turn under this allowance and slipstitch the two fabrics together.

9 Sew a small brass ring to each end of the tieback on the reverse side.

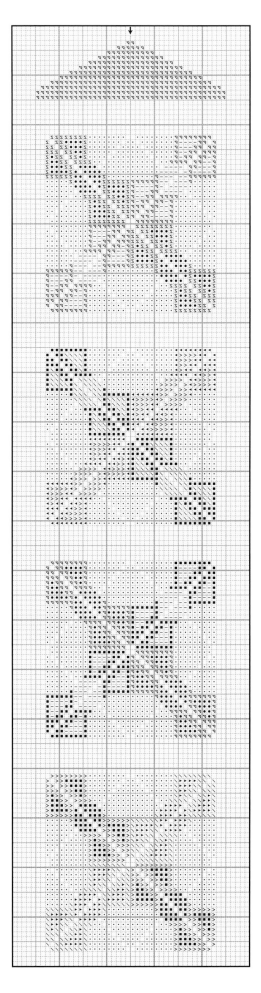

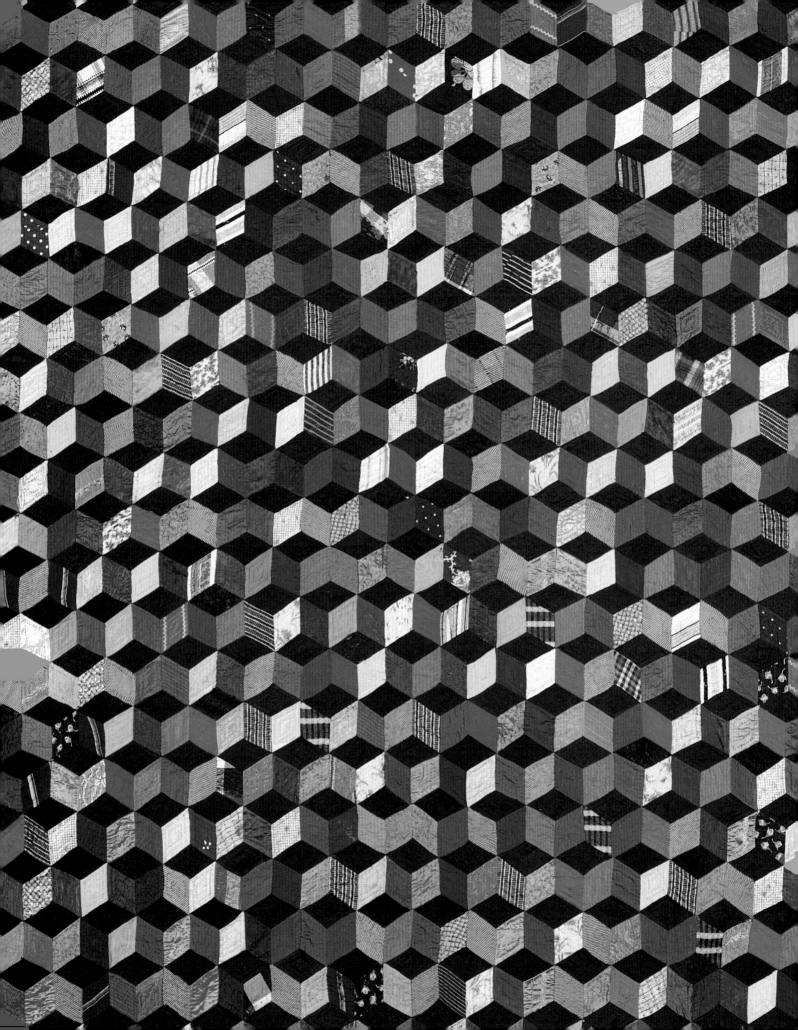

Tumbling Blocks Mirror Frame

A beautifully pieced Victorian-style quilt was the inspiration for this cross-stitch border design. The quilt is a glorious optical illusion of patterned and plain silk fabrics, possibly made from ball gowns and fancy dresses. Its effect is achieved by the careful arrangement of dark and light fabrics.

The tumbling blocks of the quilt have been translated, by the use of varied tones and metallic threads, into a subtle, modern version of the popular pattern.

Left. *Tumbling Blocks,* USA, c. 1870, 74 x 75½in, Museum Quilts Gallery, London

Finished size : 9½ x 10¾in

Stitch count : 154 x 173

MATERIALS

13¾ x 15in charcoal/dark sage Zweigart 16-count Aida (762)

10½ x 11¾in thick cardboard for window mount

Mirror and frame to fit completed mount

Tapestry needle 24

COATS ANCHOR STRANDED COTTON

(1 skein of each)

◁◁◁	234
⊟⊟	01
⦀⦀	397
⊡⊡	399
◦◦	235
▾▾	400
✳✳	403
■■	1040
⁄⁄	8581
◦◦	273
▽▽	1041
∈∈	900

KREINIK BLENDING FILAMENT / STRANDED COTTON

⬚⬚	K001HL / 399
⊞⊞	K011HL / 400
⧨⧨	K005 / 403

⊡⊡	K085 / 1041
⊞⊞	K085 / 8581
++	K085 / 273
⧀⧀	K025 / 400
╲╲	K032 / 397
ИИ	K025 / 235
∧∧	K001 / 234
⠿	K001 / 01

STITCHES AND STRANDS

Cross stitch, using 2 strands of cotton

Cross stitch, using 2 strands of cotton plus 1 strand of blending filament

WORKING THE EMBROIDERY

1 Find the center of the Aida fabric by folding into four. Tack along the folds. Attach the Aida to your stitching frame, following the instructions on page 117, and tensioning the fabric carefully.

2 Find the center of the chart by counting squares, and mark with a pencil cross. Count out from the center point to the inner edge of the border, on the chart, and do the same on the fabric. Start stitching at this point, following the chart.

3 When working with cotton and blending filament, work with fairly short lengths of the blending filament. (see page 118)

4 When the embroidery is completed, check for mistakes and loose ends, and, if necessary, press gently on the wrong side, onto a soft towel.

TO MAKE UP THE MIRROR FRAME

1 To make up the mount, follow the instructions on page 122, or take the finished work to a reputable framer.

Tumbling Blocks Beaded Box

The tumbling blocks design seemed to be highly appropriate for a box top, and I have added small glass beads to heighten the three-dimensional effect. Based on the same quilt as used for the mirror frame, this box is worked on the larger-scale, 14-count Aida, giving a good example of how designs can be changed by varying the scale of the fabric.

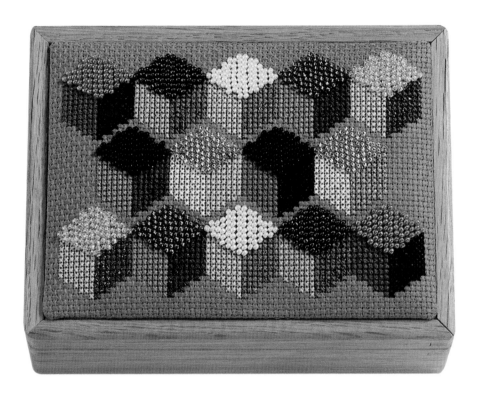

By extending the rows in either or both directions, this design can be adapted to fit most sizes of box top. Quantities are given for the box shown. If you have a different size, remember to allow extra fabric for turnings. If you are planning to extend the design, you will need graph paper to plan your own design.

The beading makes it necessary to use a slate or roller frame when stitching

this design; the size of the frame will depend upon the size of your box.

SKILL LEVEL

Finished size of embroidery : 5 x 3½in
Stitch count : 70 x 47

MATERIALS

7½ x 9in charcoal/dark sage Zweigart 14-count Aida

Box lid 4 x 6in (see page 128 for suppliers)

Piece of cardboard slightly smaller than the rebate on the box lid

Piece of light weight wadding, the same size as the card

Double-sided tapestry tape

Tapestry needle 24

Beading needle

COATS ANCHOR STRANDED
COTTON / KREINIK BLENDING
FILAMENT

(1 skein of each)

⊟	01
⫲	234
⫽	235 / K025
⊙	397
▽	400
▲	403 / K005
∶	900
■	1040
▫	1041 / K085
◇	273 / K085
✳	8581
⋊	234 / K032
╲	399 / K001
△	400 / K011HL
▽	8581 / K085

MILL HILL GLASS SEED BEADS

(1 pack of each color)

⊘	00479
＋	00161
⫽	00150
И	00081
∧	02014
I	02010
▼	02022

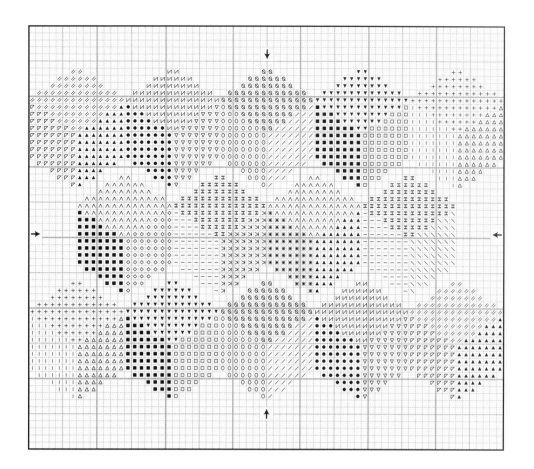

STITCHES AND STRANDS

Cross stitch, using 2 strands of cotton

Cross stitch, using 2 strands of cotton
plus 1 strand of blending filament

Use 1 strand of Anchor thread to
match the beads

WORKING THE EMBROIDERY

1 Find the center of the Aida fabric by
folding into four. Mark the center of
the fabric with a pin and tack along
the folds. Attach the fabric to your
frame following the instructions on
page 117, tensioning the fabric carefully.

2 Find the center of the charted area
by counting the squares, and mark
with a pencil cross. Start stitching
from this point, following the chart.

3 Work all the cross stitch before
adding the beads. To work with blending filament, follow the instructions on
page 118.

4 Attach the beads, using a beading
needle and 1 strand of matching cotton.

5 When the embroidery is completed,
remove from the frame, and if necessary, press gently on the wrong side,
onto a soft towel.

MAKING UP THE BOX

1 Attach the wadding to the piece of
cardboard with double-sided tapestry
tape.

2 Stretch the embroidery over the
cardboard, following the instructions
given on page 122, and secure with
double-sided tapestry tape.

3 Position the covered panel in the
box lid, following the manufacturer's
instructions.

Log Cabin Chessboard

A Log Cabin quilt is pieced from narrow strips of fabric, and sewn in different arrangements of dark and light around a small central square. The design has many variations and this particular variation, called Light and Dark, seemed a perfect choice for the contrasting squares of a chessboard. Worked in subtle colors with the addition of gold and silver kid leather, it makes an eye-catching table top or game board.

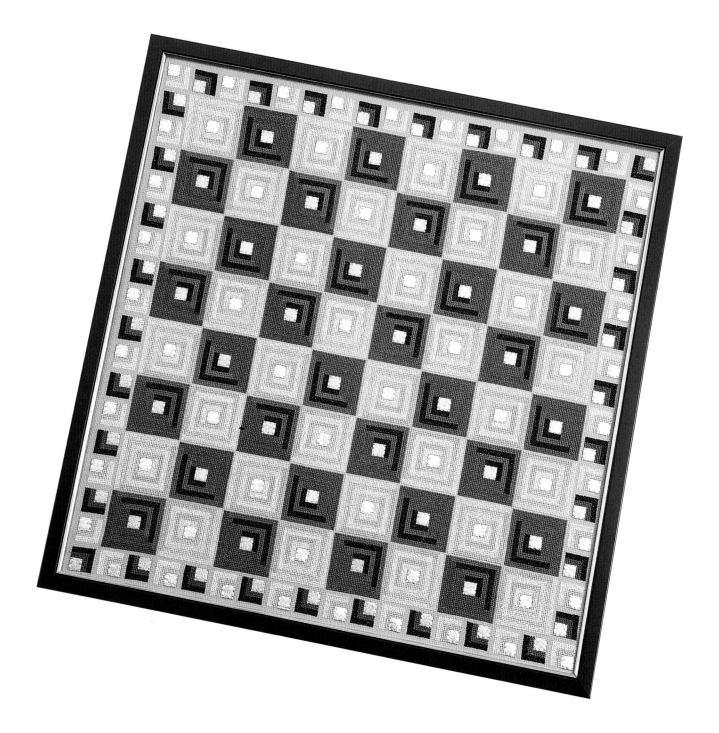

It is advisable to use a slate or roller frame for stitching this project.

SKILL LEVEL

Size: 20½ x 20½in

Stitch count: 286 x 286

MATERIALS

26 x 26in sage green /celadon Zweigart 14-count Aida (611)

21 x 21in backing board

6 x 6in gold kid leather

6 x 6in silver kid leather

Pale gray machine thread

Pale gold machine thread

Strong thread for stretching

Tapestry needle 24

Sharps or crewel needle 10

Craft knife

Metal ruler

COATS ANCHOR STRANDED COTTON

(with number of skeins)

⊟	01 x 5
⊞	851 x 6
⊡	1041 x 6
⊡	403 x 5
⊞	273 x 5
⊞	231 x 5
⊠	274 x 6
⊡	1037 x 6

STITCHES AND STRANDS

Cross stitch, using 2 strands of cotton

WORKING THE EMBROIDERY

1 Find the center of the fabric by folding in four, and tack along the folds in both directions. Attach the Aida to your stitching frame following the instructions on page 117, tensioning the fabric carefully.

2 The chart shows one half of the design. Find the center of the whole chart and mark with a pencil cross. Start stitching from the center, turning the chart through 180 degrees when the first half has been completed. Work all the cross stitch before applying the kid leather.

MAKING UP THE CHESSBOARD

1 The squares marked with a cross on the chart indicate the position of the kid leather squares. Cut sixty-six ½in squares from the gold kid leather, and the same from the silver leather, using a sharp craft knife and a metal ruler. Stitch in place, using machine thread, and small, evenly spaced stitches.

2 Check for mistakes and loose ends. If required, press on the wrong side onto a soft towel.

3 To stretch the embroidery over the board, follow the instructions given on page 122. It is recommended that a piece of work of this size should be taken to a professional framer for glazing and framing.

Log Cabin, Light and Dark Variation
USA, c. 1930, 78 x 92in, Museum Quilts Gallery, London

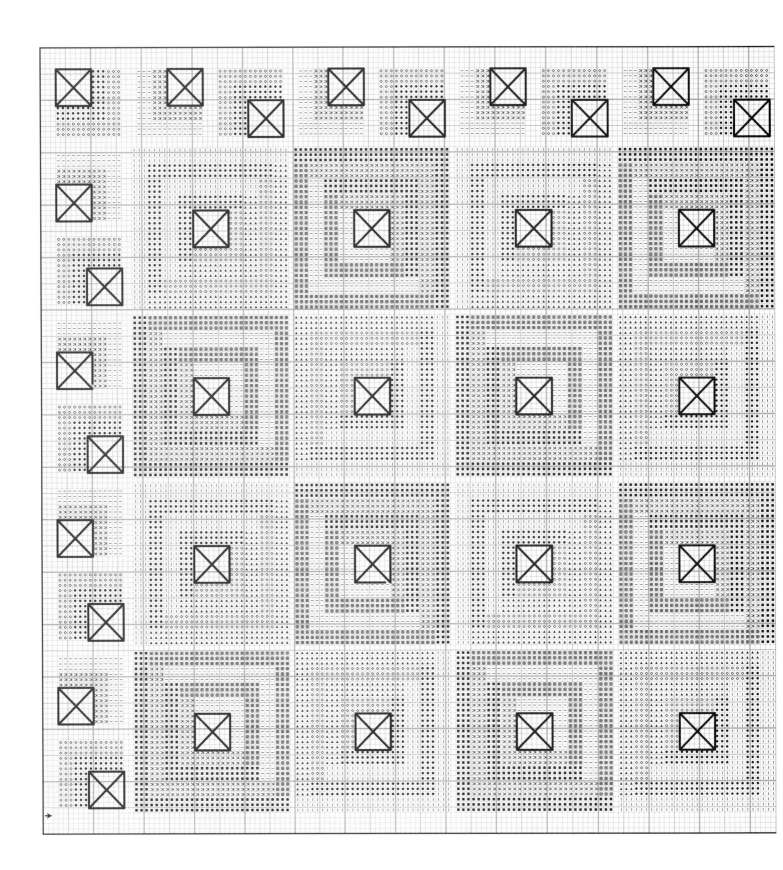

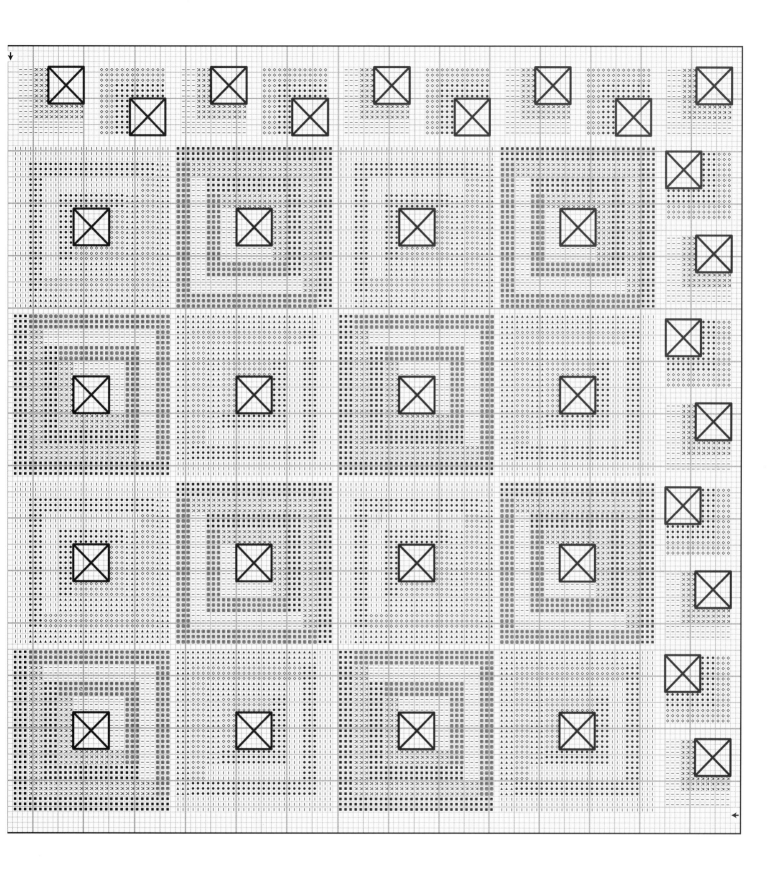

Album Quilt, New Jersey, USA, c. 1862, 80 x 90in, Museum Quilts Gallery, London

Rose Garland Picture

This project, and the pincushions and tray which follow, are based on motifs from a remarkable album quilt made largely by members of the Ketcham family in New Jersey, in 1862. Each block of the quilt is composed of a different motif, and several blocks are inscribed in indelible ink with sayings, poems, and biblical references, and signed "from your mother," "from your cousin," etc. There is some speculation that the quilt was made for a son who was going off to war. The fabrics used are fine chintzes, plain and glazed cottons, often featuring intricate trapunto. There is elaborate gold thread work to pick out details.

This garland, composed of appliquéd full-blown roses, buds, and leaves, translates very happily into counted cross stitch. The aged, faded look of the quilt is achieved by a choice of soft colors, and by using backstitch very sparingly.

SKILL LEVEL

Finished size of worked area: 6½ x 6in

Stitch count : 89 x 85

MATERIALS

12 x 12in oyster-pink/bisque Zweigart
14-count Aida (302)

9 x 9in backing board

9 x 9in mount in a complementary
color, with a 7in diameter window

Picture frame to fit

Tapestry needle 24

COATS ANCHOR STRANDED
COTTON

(1 skein of each)

			1009
◇ ◇	868
S S	1013
● ●	1020
▬ ▬	1022
◲	1024

◪	19
◿	897
◹ ◹	875
✳ ✳	877
∧ ∧	879

BACKSTITCH

403

879

897

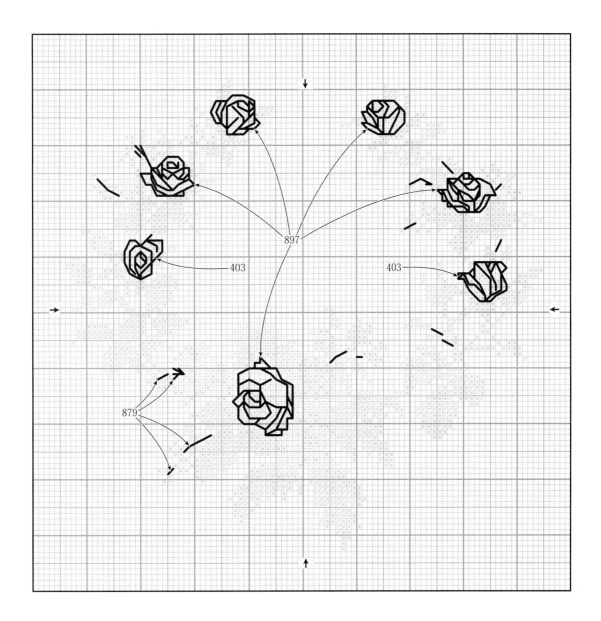

STITCHES AND STRANDS

Cross stitch, using 2 strands of cotton

Backstitch, using 1 strand of cotton, in 403 and 897

Backstitch, using 2 strands of cotton, in 879

WORKING THE EMBROIDERY

1 Find the center of the Aida fabric by folding into four. Find the center of the charted area by counting the squares. Mark the center of the fabric with a pin and the center of the chart with a pencil cross.

2 Count from the central cross on the chart to the nearest flower or leaf, find the matching spot on the fabric, and begin stitching there. Work all the cross stitch before adding the back-stitch details.

MAKING UP THE PICTURE

1 When the embroidery is completed, check for mistakes and loose threads, and press gently on the wrong side, onto a soft towel.

2 To mount the garland, follow the instructions given on page 122, or take it to a reputable framer for mounting and framing.

Beaded Pincushions

This smart trio of beaded pincushions depicting berries, an arum lily, and a garland is based on appliqué panels in the album quilt on page 72. Though each design is different, with its own border and tassel or loop decoration, the crisp red and green color scheme unites them into a pleasing set, of more interest than if they had been exactly the same.

The quantities given are for all three pincushions, but you might want to make just one as a gift. The tassel or loop decorations are optional.

SKILL LEVEL

Finished size : 6 x 6in

Stitch count : 81 x 81 (garland), 83 x 83 (berries and arum lily)

MATERIALS

Three 7 x 7in squares of ivory Zweigart 16-count Aida (264)

Three 7 x 7in squares of fine patterned cotton

Polyester stuffing

Strip of cardboard 1½in, for tassels

Tapestry needle 26

Beading needle 10

COATS ANCHOR STRANDED COTTON

(with number of skeins)

⊞	46 x 1
⊞	20 x 1
⧄	1044 x 2

 262 x 1

 00165

MILL HILL GLASS BEADS

(1 box of each color)

00165 seed beads

05025 pebble beads

STITCHES AND STRANDS

Cross stitch, using 2 strands of cotton

Backstitch (1044) using 1 strand of cotton

WORKING THE EMBROIDERY

1 Find the center of the chart by counting and the center of the fabric by folding into four. Starting from the center, stitch the cross-stitch areas, following the chart.

2 Work the border, counting out from the center very carefully to position it correctly (the number of blank squares is not the same for each design).

3 Add the beads to the cross-stitch area, using one strand of 46, and stitching in the same direction each time (see page 120).

Garland

Berries

Arum Lily

MAKING UP THE PINCUSHION

1 Place the Aida right sides together with a piece of patterned cotton, which forms the back. Stitch along the four sides, ¼in from the border, leaving part of one side open for stuffing.

2 Trim the seams to ¼in from the seam. Turn right sides out, press lightly and stuff carefully.

3 Stitch up the opening using ladder stitch. (see page 121)

To make the thread tassels, as on the garland pincushion, follow the instructions on page 126, using stranded cotton 46 and a piece of cardboard 1½in wide.

Make four small tassels, bind them with the same color, and take the thread at the top of the tassel through a glass pebble bead before it is attached to the corner of the pincushion.

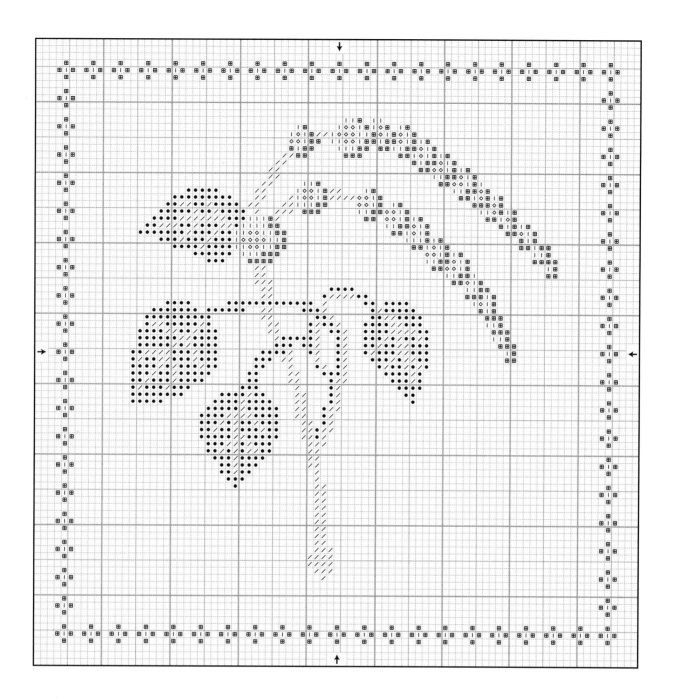

To make the beaded tassels, as on the berries pincushion, thread ten seed beads, one pebble bead and finally one seed bead onto a matching thread. Take the needle back through the large bead and the ten small ones to form a tassel. Take both ends of the thread through another pebble bead before stitching to the corner of the pincushion.

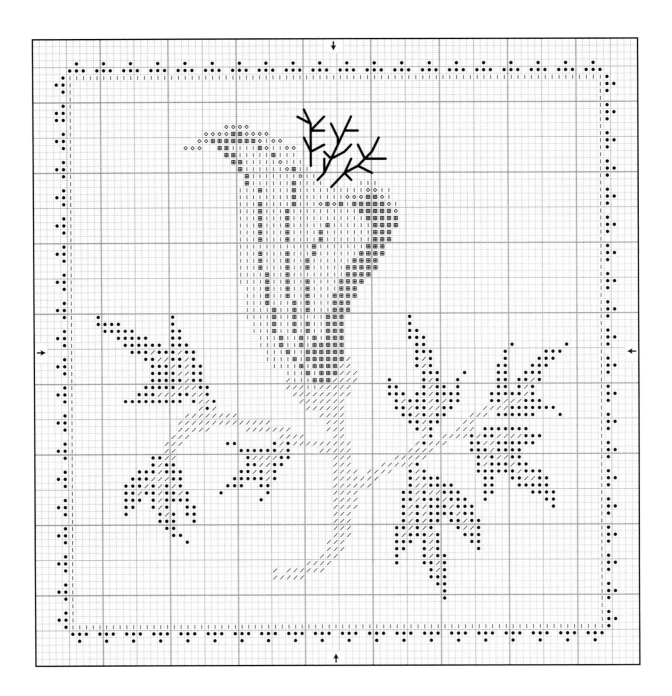

To make the beaded loops, as on the arum-lily pincushion, thread twenty seed beads onto a matching thread, and tie to make a loop, but do not cut the thread. Thread a further twenty beads onto the thread and tie off as before. Take the two ends through a pebble bead before attaching to the corner of the pincushion.

Floral Bouquet Tray

A bold, colorful posy of flowers and berries from the Album quilt on page 72 was the starting point for this design. Used here on a small tray, it would look equally effective framed as a small picture or repeated several times to make a cushion.

SKILL LEVEL

Finished size : 4¾ x 5in

Stitch count : 67 x 69

MATERIALS

13 x 13in white Zweigart 14-count Aida

9 x 9in mount, with 5½ x 5½in circular window

9 x 9in Sudberry House small square tray

Adhesive tape, or strong thread for lacing

Tapestry needle 24

COATS ANCHOR STRANDED COTTON

(1 skein of each)

⊞	35
✳	46
▼	891
+	1017
◦	1019
◦	873
◫	972
◙	76
∴	859
◼	861
≡	862
и	683
⋊	877

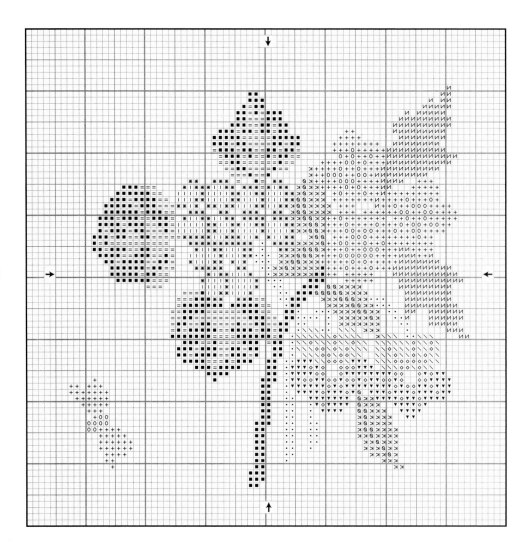

BACKSTITCH

403

873

859

STITCHES AND STRANDS

Cross stitch, using 2 strands of stranded cotton.

Backstitch, using 1 strand (403) of stranded cotton for flowers and butterfly, 2 strands (873) for berries, 1 strand (859) for tendrils, and 2 strands (859) for leaf veins on right side.

WORKING THE EMBROIDERY

1 Find the center of the Aida by folding it into four, and the center of the chart by counting the squares.

2 Mark the center of the fabric with a pin and the center of the chart with a pencil cross.

3 Counting out from the center, work the embroidery, following the chart, and making sure the design is centered. When the stitching is complete, press gently on the back onto a soft towel.

MAKING UP THE TRAY

1 Unscrew the four brass screws in the tray and carefully slide out the glass, mounting board and the base of the tray.

2 Wrap the Aida around the mounting board and secure it at the back with tape, or lace from side to side for a firm fit.

3 Clean the glass and reassemble the tray, placing the mount over the embroidery.

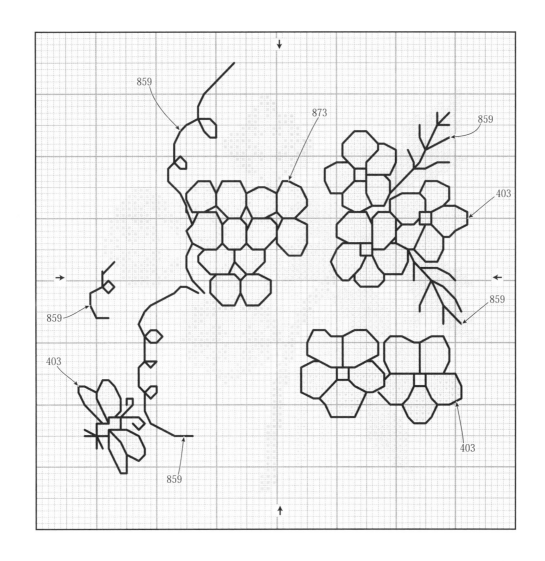

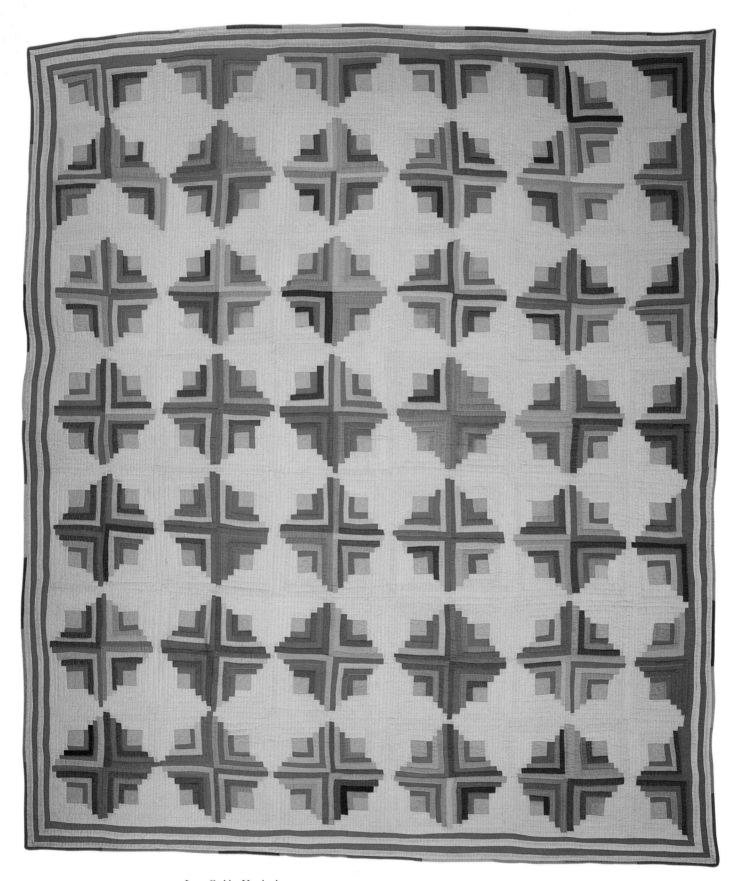

Log Cabin Variation, USA, c. 1930, 78 x 92in, Museum Quilts Gallery, London

Log Cabin Cushion with Zigzag Border

This project uses the bold red, yellow, and green design of a Log Cabin quilt made in 1930, which, with very little adaptation, is superb for cross stitch. Each quilt block is half dark and half light, and the overall design is achieved by arranging the blocks to create diamond shapes. The border of the cushion is based on a mistake on the original quilt, where patches have been assembled in the wrong order, creating a zigzag rather than a block.

Finished size: 16 x 16in

Stitch count : 198 x 198

MATERIALS

18 x 18in white Zweigart 14-count
Aida

18 x 18in Christmas-green 28-count
Jobelan (NJ429 43 140) for backing

16 x 16in cushion pad

Tapestry needle 24

COATS ANCHOR STRANDED
COTTON

(4 skeins of each)

⊞	46
⊡	302
⊠	244

STITCHES AND STRANDS

Cross stitch, using 2 strands of cotton

WORKING THE EMBROIDERY

1 Find the center of the Aida fabric
by folding into four. Find the center
of the charted area by counting the
squares. Mark the center of the fabric with a pin and the center of the
chart with a pencil cross.

2 Start by stitching the outer border, counting out from the center.
This will help with the positioning
of the inner motifs. Count the blank
squares between the motifs carefully, as the spacing is not always the
same.

MAKING UP THE CUSHION

1 When the embroidery is completed, tack stitch a square measuring
16 x 16in around the outside of the
worked area, making sure that the
center point of this square matches
exactly the center point of the
worked area. This square marks the
edges of the finished cushion and
will act as a stitching guide.

2 Check for mistakes and loose
threads, and press gently on the
wrong side, onto a soft towel.

3 To make up the cushion, follow
the instructions given on page 124.

Pastel Log Cabin Cushion

This variation on the previous Log Cabin cushion is based on the same quilt, shown on page 86. The clean, bright colors of the quilt, and the way they are used, suggest the look of a child's coloring patterns, which prompted me to heighten this effect in my cross-stitch adaptation. So, this cushion has inner diamonds "drawn" in backstitch on crisp white Aida, with a border of small randomly colored squares representing the beginning of the "coloring in."

Finished size : 16 x 16in

Stitch count : 182 x 182

MATERIALS

18 x 18in white Zweigart 14-count
Aida

18 x 18in fine gray glazed cotton

16 x 16in cushion pad

Stiff card, 3in wide

Tapestry needle 24

COATS ANCHOR STRANDED
COTTON

(with number of skeins)

	46 x 2	
	302 x 2	
	244 x 1	
	323 x 1	
	25 x 1	
	206 x 1	
	186 x 1	
	161 x 1	
	131 x 1	
	1016 x 1	

BACKSTITCH

398 x 6 (inc. 4 skeins for
optional tassels)

STITCHES AND STRANDS

Cross stitch, using 2 strands of cotton

Backstitch, using 2 strands of cotton

WORKING THE EMBROIDERY

1 Find the center of the Aida fabric
by folding into four. Find the center
of the charted area by counting the
squares. Mark the center of the fabric
with a pin and the center of the chart
with a pencil cross.

2 Start by stitching the outer border,
counting out from the center. This
will help with the positioning of the
inner backstitch areas. Try not to run
colors from one area to another, as
they will tend to show through the
fabric when the cushion pad is
inserted.

MAKING UP THE CUSHION

1 When the embroidery is completed,
tack stitch a square measuring 16 x
16in around the outside of the worked
area, making sure that the center
point of this square matches exactly
the center point of the worked area.
This square marks the edges of the
finished cushion and will act as a
stitching guide.

2 Check for mistakes and loose
threads, and press gently on the wrong
side, onto a soft towel.

3 To make up the cushion and the
tassels, follow the instructions given
on pages 124-126.

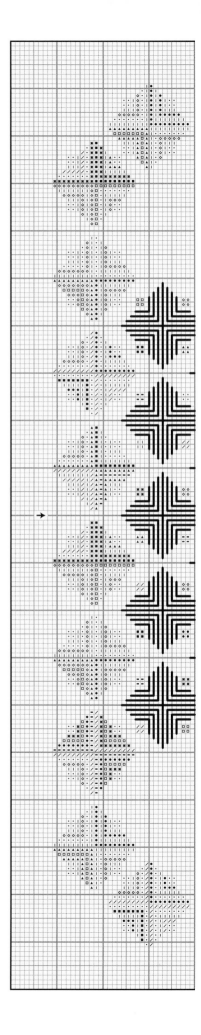

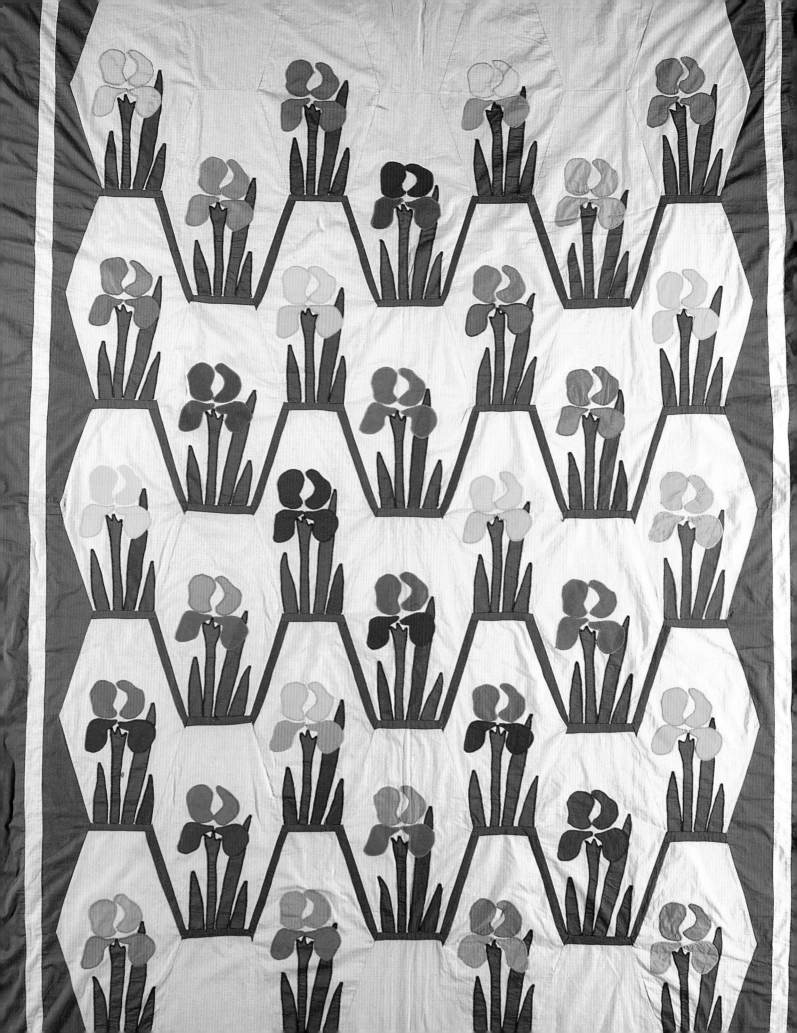

Art Deco Iris Window Screen

Based on Ruby Short McKim's Art Deco Iris quilt, this delicately colored window screen uses a combination of cross-stitch and hardanger embroidery on white linen bands of two different widths. The bands hang from a curtain pole, making a subtle treatment for a whole window where privacy is important, or they could be used to cover just the bottom half of the window, like café curtains. The clever construction means that you can easily adjust the length to fit any window (by changing the length of the bands) or adjust the width (by having more or fewer bands).

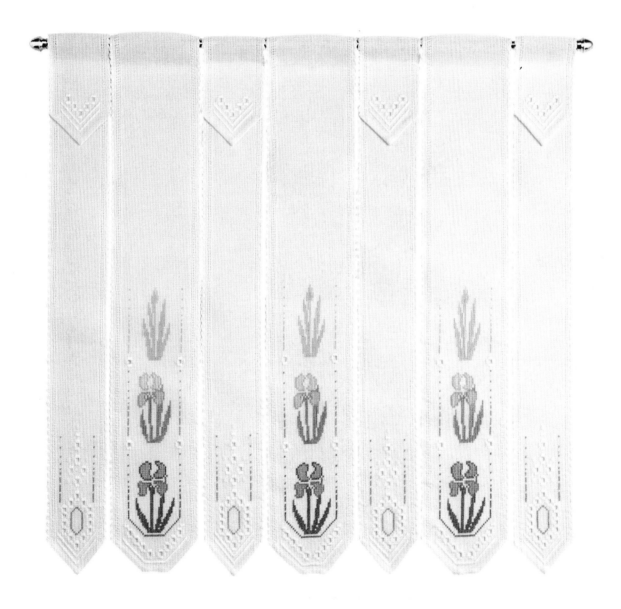

Left. *Iris Quilt*, USA, c. 1920, 96 x 78in, Museum Quilts Gallery, London

Quantities will vary according to the size of your window.

Note that you will need a greater quantity of thread number 01, which is used for the hardanger. The screen shown uses seven bands.

SKILL LEVEL

Finished size to fit window

Stitch count: including hardanger borders. Narrow band: top 22 x 24, bottom 22 x 72

Broad band: 39 x 158

MATERIALS

White Zweigart scalloped-edge linen bands in two widths: 3in (E7272), and 4¾in (E7273)

Decoupage or papercraft scissors, for cutting hardanger stitches

Tapestry needle 24

Fine curtain pole to fit window

COATS ANCHOR STRANDED COTTON

(1 skein of each)

▦	875
▨	876
▤	1042
▧	870
▨	872
◉	117
✶	118
▾	90
▨	103

 120

01 (hardanger) x 3 skeins

STITCHES AND STRANDS

Cross stitch, using 2 strands of cotton, worked over 2 x 2 threads of the fabric

Hardanger, using 3 strands of cotton, worked over 4 threads of the fabric

WORKING THE EMBROIDERY

1 First, measure your window to find the finished length and width of the screen, then calculate the required number of both types of band, and thus the total quantity of each width of linen band. For each of the narrower bands, the length of linen band required is the finished length of the screen plus 7½in to allow for the embroidery at the top. For each of the wider bands, with the iris motifs, the length of linen band required is the finished length of the screen plus 3in.

2 For the narrower band, start the hardanger stitching in the center of the band, 1in from the bottom. Each hardanger block is made up of five stitches (see page 120). The outlined squares on the chart indicate the position of the hardanger blocks (see page 120). Take care to finish off any ends of embroidery thread securely, and as invisibly as possible.

3 Add the cross stitch, following the chart, noting that the black outlined shapes on the chart give the position of the hardanger blocks.

4 Cut the centers from the hardanger crosses very carefully, referring to the chart. The squares filled with a star indicate the squares to be removed.

MAKING UP THE CURTAIN

1 For the bottom hem, make a diagonal fold ½in from the last line of stitching. Trim ½in from this fold. Fold and cut the other side of the

band to match. Make a narrow hem from the folded over fabric, mitering the center point. Stitch as invisibly as possible.

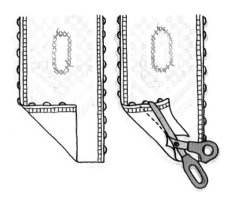

2 With the right side of the band facing, fold over the top 6½in of the band onto the right side (avoid creasing the fold at this stage). Starting in the center, 1in from the end of the band, work the top section of the embroidery. Finish the top by making a narrow pointed hem to match the bottom.

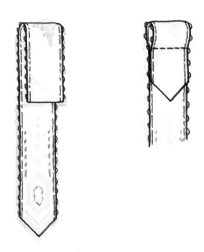

3 Press carefully on the wrong side of the stitching, onto a soft towel. Press the top fold 6in from the mitered top edge.

4 Backstitch across the width of the band, 1½in from the fold to make a

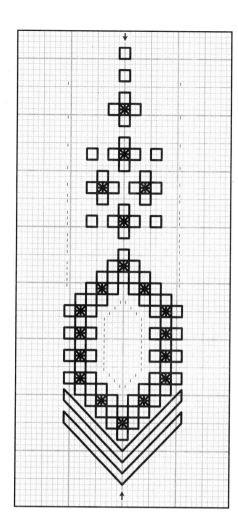

channel for the curtain pole. (Before stitching, check that the pole will fit this channel, and adjust the width if necessary.)

5 For the wider band, turn under the top 2in of the band, then turn under ½in of this to make a narrow hem, and backstitch across the width of the band to make a channel for the pole. Adjust the width of the channel if necessary to match the channel on the narrower band.

6 Complete the embroidery, following the chart, then complete the bottom hem as for the narrower band. Press carefully on the wrong side onto a soft towel.

7 Stitch the required number of both types of band to fit your window and arrange them on the pole alternately.

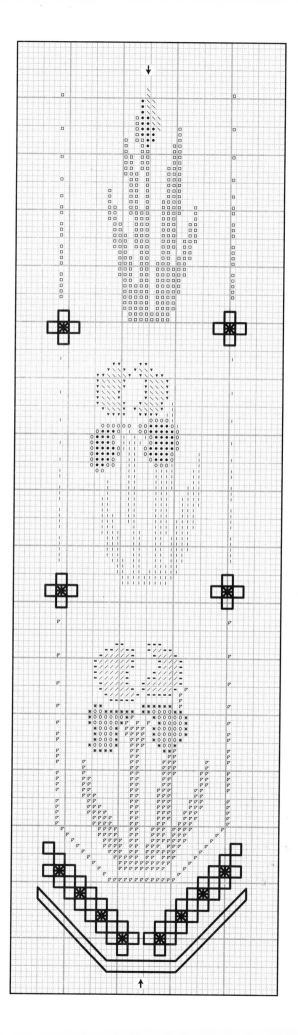

Art Deco Iris Handtowel

In real life, the stylized irises on this Art Deco quilt are unexpectedly large, but they reduce down very successfully for simple cross stitch. On this green handtowel, in shades of blue and purple, they look modern and cheerful—perfect for a cloakroom or as a guest towel, perhaps with matching bath towel. If you are feeling adventurous, the iris motif could also be used as a stencil motif to decorate the walls and lend a co-ordinated look.

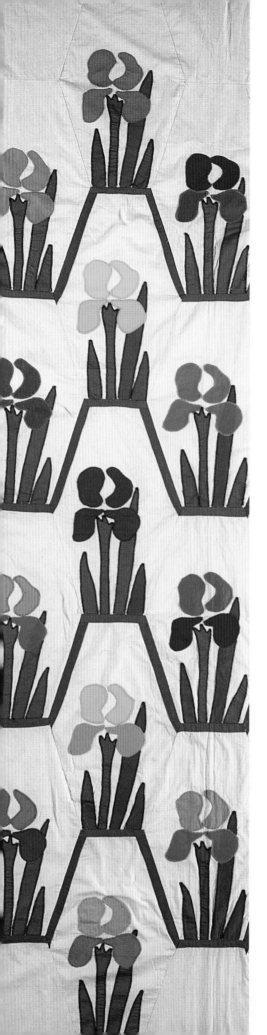

Finished size of worked area (on towel shown): 9 x 2in

Stitch count (each motif): 24 x 27, plus 1 stitch between motifs

MATERIALS

10½ x 18in Charles Craft Seafoam handtowel

Tapestry needle 24

COATS ANCHOR STRANDED COTTON

(1 skein of each)

⊟	879	⊠	118
⊞	851	⊞	142
✳	119	⊞	101

STITCHES AND STRANDS

Cross stitch, using 2 strands of cotton

WORKING THE EMBROIDERY

1 Find the center of the band on the towel. Find the center of the charted area by counting the squares. Mark the center of the fabric with a pin and the center of the chart with a pencil cross.

2 Starting from the center, stitch the dark green zigzag line which encloses the irises, and then work the irises themselves. Take care not to pull the thread too tight, as the blockweave band is not as firm as conventional Aida fabric.

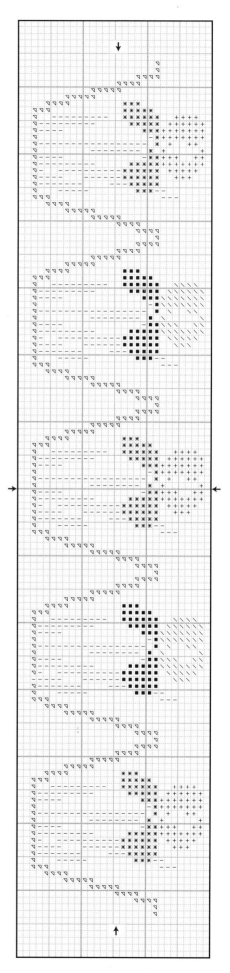

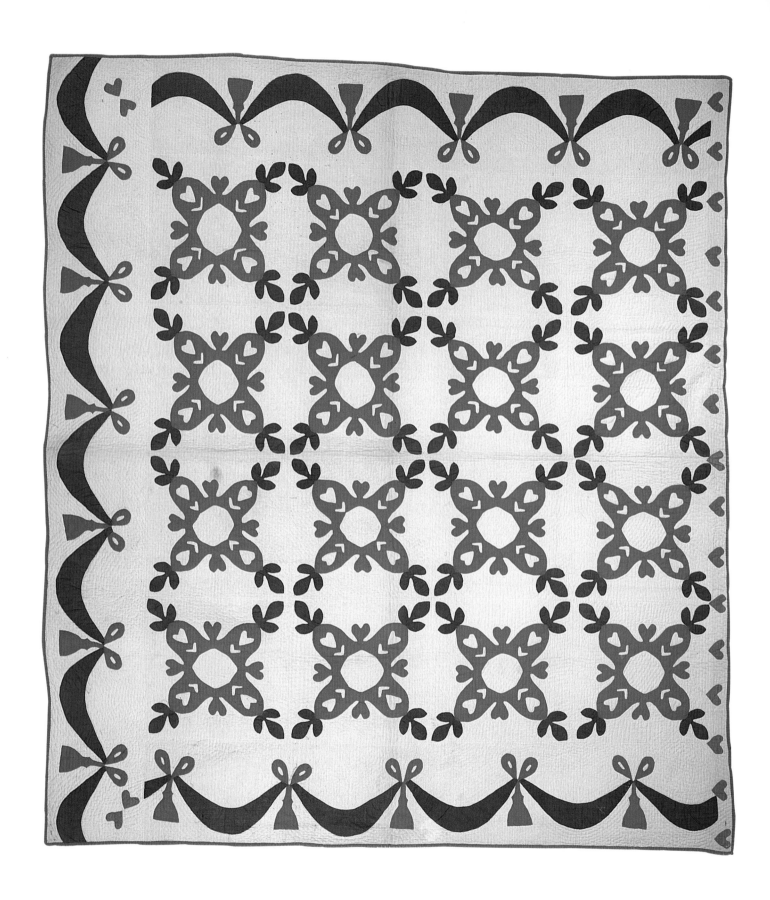

Folk Art Marriage Quilt, Pennsylvania, USA, c. 1860, 75 x 84in, Museum Quilts Gallery, London

Folk Art Backgammon Board

The Folk Art Marriage quilt which inspired this project comes from Pennsylvania, and dates from around 1860. Its red, green, and white color scheme is traditional, but its delightful character is largely the result of unique design features, such as the red hearts cut out of the interior motifs, and the irregularity of the swags, tassels, and leaves. I have organized these motifs into the normal layout of a backgammon board, supplementing the original colors with gold and silver to give added richness. The rather impressive result makes an ideal Christmas gift.

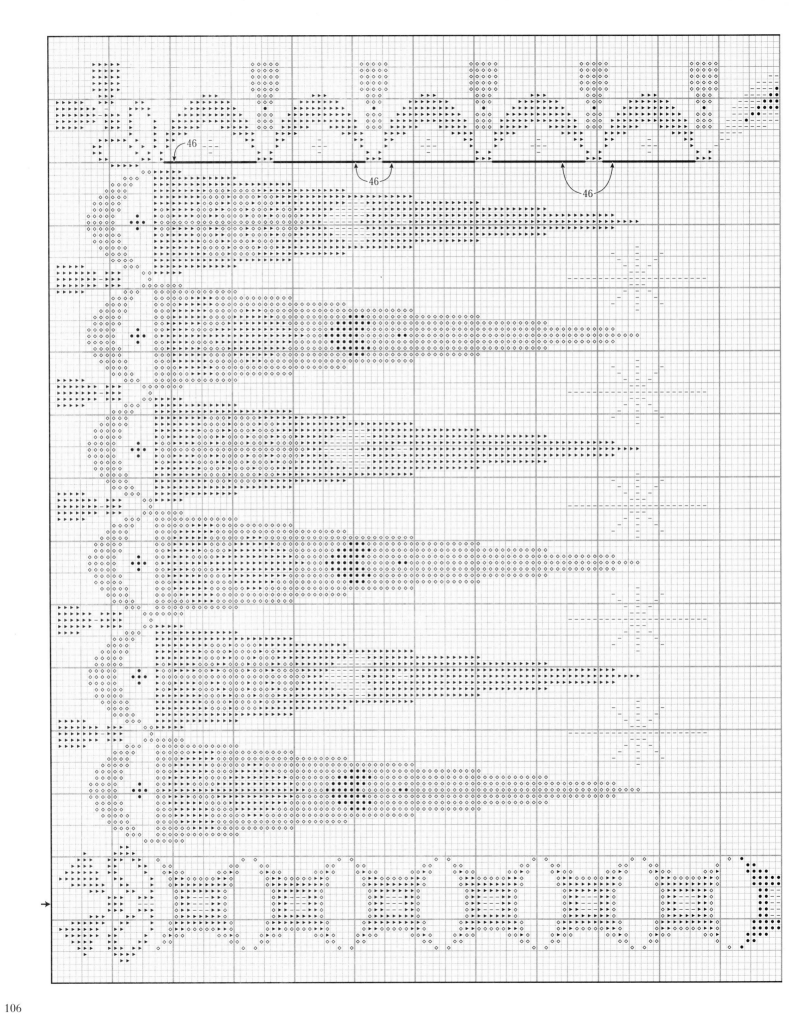

The chart shows one half of the backgammon board plus the center band. To complete the design, turn the chart through 180 degrees, so that the quarters match diagonally. When working this design, I recommend using a rectangular roller frame of a suitable size, which helps to control the tension of the stitches, especially with the metal threads.

SKILL LEVEL

Finished size (worked area): 17 x 20in

Stitch count: 239 x 271

MATERIALS

24 x 28in white Zweigart 14-count Aida

Tapestry needle 24

COATS ANCHOR STRANDED COTTON

(4 skeins of each)

⣿	001 (silver)	
⊞	862 (gold)	

KREINIK VERY FINE BRAID #4

(2 spools of each)

⦂	46	
▶▶	246	

STITCHES AND STRANDS

Cross stitch, using 2 strands of cotton

Backstitch, using 2 strands of cotton

WORKING THE EMBROIDERY

1 Find the center of the fabric by folding into four and find the center of the chart by counting squares.

2 Start stitching from the center and work the center band of square motifs.

3 Complete the rest of the cross stitch, then the backstitch, following the chart. Remember to turn the chart 180 degrees to work the second half.

4 Remove from the frame, check for mistakes and loose stitches, and press on the wrong side onto a soft towel.

MAKING UP THE BOARD

1 If you wish to stretch the embroidery and make up the board yourself, see page 122. Otherwise, take it to a reputable professional framer and ask him to stretch, frame and mount it under glass, as for a picture (allowing clearance so that the glass is not touching the embroidery).

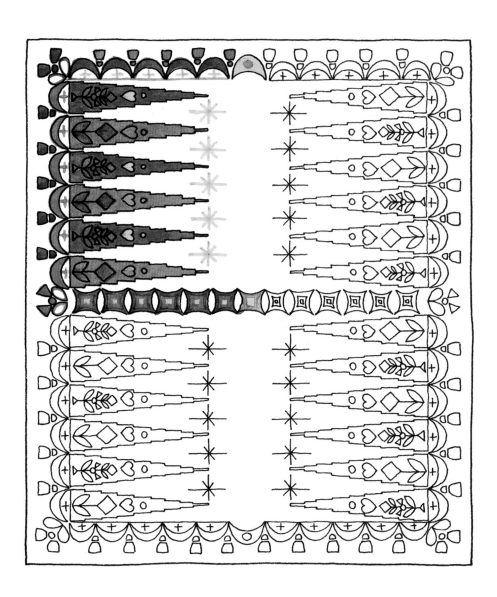

Folk Art
Christmas Tree Decorations

Based on motifs from two early folk-art quilts from Pennsylvania, these decorations would add color and glitter to even the smallest Christmas tree.

I have made three decorations from each of the red and green linen bands, but you could, of course, choose which you would like to make, and perhaps adapt the colors and motifs to your own scheme. The designs would look equally good on Aida bands of the same width. Note that the linen bands are not cut into individual decorations until after all the motifs have been stitched.

SKILL LEVEL

Finished size:
Decoration A 3 x 4½in
Decoration B 3 x 4in
Decoration C 3 x 3½in
Decoration D 3 x 3¾in
Decoration E 3 x 4½in
Decoration F 3 x 4½in

Stitch count: A - 57 x 29, B - 51 x 29,
C - 44 x 29, D - 47 x 29, E - 57 x 29,
F - 57 x 29

MATERIALS

1yd Frankfurter Handarbeiten linen
band in each of red/green (0908-20),
red/gold (0908-30), green/red (0908-
21) and green/gold (0908-31)

1yd Vilene craft pelmet interlining
(H1840) or Pellon extra-heavy
stabilizer (No 65)

Stiff cardboard, 3in wide

4yd green and red ⅛in wide satin ribbon, cut into 8in lengths

Tapestry needle 24

COATS ANCHOR STRANDED
COTTON

(with number of skeins)

 01 x 2

245 x 3

46 x 3

KREINIK VERY FINE BRAID #4

001 (silver) x 2

002 (gold) x 4

STITCHES AND STRANDS

Cross stitch, using 2 strands of cotton,
or one strand of metallic thread
worked over 2 x 2 fabric threads.

WORKING THE EMBROIDERY

1 Find the center of the linen band
and the center of the charted motifs
by counting. Start stitching from the
center, ½in from the end of the band.
Stitch all three motifs on each band,
allowing 1in between each motif.

MAKING UP THE DECORATIONS

1 Cut the band into individual decorations, then cut the remaining band
into backing pieces, the same size as
the worked pieces.

2 Place backing and worked piece
right sides together and stitch the bottom seam ¼in from the embroidery.
Trim to within ¼in. Turn right sides
out and press.

3 Slipstitch together the sides of the
decoration. Turn in the top edges, ¼in
from the embroidery, to match the
bottom edge. Press, open out and trim
turnover to ¼in from the fold.

4 Cut interlining slightly smaller than
the decoration, and insert inside the
decoration. Slipstitch the top edge
closed, catching in the length of ribbon at the point to make a loop.

5 Make a small tassel for each decoration (see page 126) from matching or
contrasting cotton, binding the tassel
with silver or gold thread. Attach tassel
to bottom point, with neat stitches on
the back.

Red bands

Green bands

Folk Art Christmas Cards

Bold, cheerful garlands and trees in cross stitch make rather special Christmas cards. The garland comes from the Ketcham family album quilt on page 72. The original red and green color scheme of the quilt garland is perfect for Christmas, but I have also changed it to a more unusual cool cream and green on black Aida. Both are shown, so that you can make your own choice, or stitch several of each.

The design for the tree card (white "snow-covered" trees on a green background provides an eye-catching twist to the usual idea) was inspired by the simple repeated motif and striking green and mauve color scheme of an Amish evergreen quilt.

Finished size (Garland card): 3⅓in
diameter

Stitch count (Garland card): 60 x 61

Finished size (Tree card): 3½ x 3¾in

Stitch count (Tree card): 49 x 52

MATERIALS

Garland cards

6 x 6in ivory(264) or black (095)
Zweigart 18-count Aida

6 x 8in Craft Creations mounts, with
4in square or round window

Tree card

6 x 6in Christmas-green 28-count
Jobelan (NJ429 43 140)

6 x 8in Craft Creations mount, with
4in square window

Tapestry needle 26

Double-sided adhesive tape

COATS ANCHOR STRANDED
COTTON

(1 skein of each)

Red garland card

⊙⊙ / ⊙⊙	46
⊞⊞ / ⊞⊞	20
＼＼	262
•• / ••	1044
✳✳ / ✳✳	Gold

Cream garland card

++ / ++	01
▲▲ / ▲▲	300
＼＼	262
•• / ••	1044

Tree card

++ / ++	01
•• / ••	403
▱▱ / ▱▱	Silver

KREINIK JAPAN THREAD

Garland cards: Gold (002J)

Tree card: Silver (001J)

STITCHES AND STRANDS

Cross stitch, using 2 strands of cotton

Backstitch, using 1 strand of cotton,
cream garland only

WORKING THE EMBROIDERY

1 Find the center of the Aida fabric
by folding into four. Find the center of
the charted area by counting the
squares. Mark the center of the fabric
with a pin and the center of the chart
with a pencil cross.

2 Starting from the center, work all
the cross stitch, then the backstitch.

MAKING UP THE CARD

1 Check for mistakes and loose
threads, and press gently on the wrong
side, onto a soft towel.

2 To mount the cards, follow the
instructions given on page 123.

Amish Evergreen,
Ohio, USA, c. 1930, 68 x 74in, Museum Quilts Gallery, London

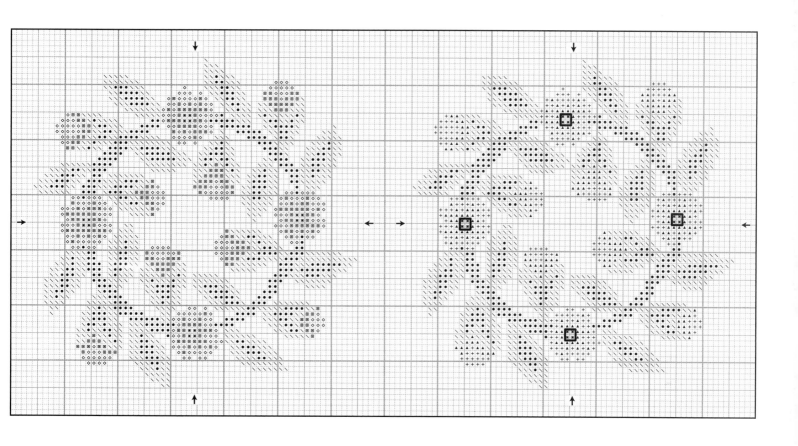

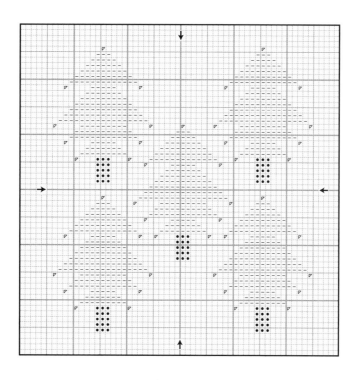

Getting Started

Equipment, Fabric and Thread

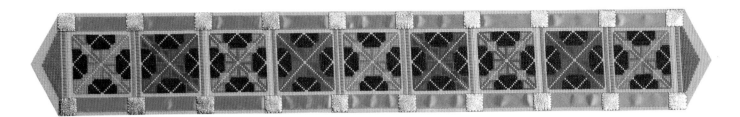

For the techniques used in this book, very little is needed in the way of equipment. As you progress and tackle new areas of the craft you will need to add to the range of threads, fabrics and other items, but for the moment the following will suffice :

Selection of tapestry, beading and Sharp needles

Fine-pointed embroidery scissors

Dressmaker's scissors

Slate or roller frame for the larger projects. These come in a variety of sizes.

Thimble

Tape measure and ruler

Thread for tacking

Good-quality dressmaker's pins

Masking tape or woven tape

Iron

Needles

TAPESTRY needles for counted cross stitch come in sizes 14–26, and have a large eye and a blunt end, which separates the threads of the fabric instead of splitting them.

SHARPS needles are, as their name suggests, fine and sharp-pointed, with a small eye. They are used for any general sewing, such as hems and sewing up cushions, and come in sizes 3–10.

BEADING needles are available in sizes 10–13, and are very long and fine. They are used for sewing beads to a project. For the projects in this book a size 10 is adequate, but you may find a size 10 crewel needle easier to handle than the very long beading needle.

Needles for counted cross stitch have longer eyes than needles for plain sewing. This makes threading one thick thread or several thin ones easier. All needles are numerically graded from fine to coarse, the higher numbers being the finer needles. Exact choice of needle is a matter of personal preference, but the eye of the needle should take the thread easily, and should be the right size to draw the thread through the fabric without distorting it.

Each project in this book will give you a specific size of needle to use, and you will soon discover by practice and "feel" which size of needle suits the fabric in question.

Frames

SLATE OR ROLLER FRAMES are rectangular stitching frames which come in a variety of sizes from 12–36in, and are essential for large, concentrated areas of stitching, as they control the tension and leave both hands free to stitch, thus speeding up the operation considerably. Some people advocate the use of a ring frame, but I prefer to avoid this method as I feel that the frame distorts the weave of the fabric, making a ring in it which can often be difficult to remove. Never use a ring frame on a large design, as this can damage the worked stitches as the frame is moved from area to area.

You may find that you can work the smaller projects in your hand, but I personally always use a frame except for very small pieces.

Fabric

Any evenweave fabric of cotton or linen, loosely or closely woven with easily counted threads, is suitable for counted cross stitch. The count relates to the number of threads or blocks to the inch, which in turn will govern the size of the cross stitches. Projects in this book have been worked on Aida, Jobelan and linen fabrics.

AIDA is available in a variety of thread counts from 11 to 18.

JOBELAN is a 28-count fabric, which is usually worked over two threads, equating to 14-count Aida.

LINEN comes in a range of thread counts from 19 to 55.

By changing the count of the fabric, from the one which is specified to one which is finer or coarser, the scale of the design can be reduced or increased. Remember that the thread quantities

Embroidery Threads

Threads come in a wide range of colors and textures. Some are used as a single thickness, while others are composed of six strands, which can be separated and put back together in differing proportions. For counted thread work the following threads are most suitable.

STRANDED COTTON comes in an extensive color range, and is a slightly shiny, six-strand thread which is very adaptable.

PEARL or PERLE COTTON is a 2-ply thread which is more lustrous than stranded cotton and cannot be split. It comes in four sizes, 3, 5, 8 and 12. Size 5 relating to a 22-count evenweave fabric.

COTON à BRODER is a single-thickness thread, softer than stranded or pearl cotton and not as lustrous. It is available in a range of sizes, size 16 relating to a 28-count evenweave fabric.

BLENDING FILAMENT is a 1-ply flat reflecting filament twisted with a plain fiber. It comes in a great variety of colors and metallics and is usually used, along with several strands of stranded cotton, to give sparkle to a design.

METALLIC THREADS come in a vast range of thicknesses. Many are not suitable for cross stitch, but, by choosing carefully and reading the manufacturer's recommendations, several can be found which will stand up to being pulled repeatedly through the fabric.

Preparing the Fabric

To ensure a satisfactory result, follow these simple instructions before starting to work your embroidery.

First, press your fabric, using a steam iron, or a dry iron and a damp cloth, to remove any creases. Cut the fabric to size, as indicated in the project, and oversew the edge by machine or by hand to prevent fraying.

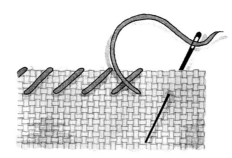

Masking tape is an alternative way of binding the edge, but this can make the piece rather difficult to handle.

Marking the Center of the Fabric

To ensure that the design is placed centrally on the fabric, use the following method. If the design is a complete unit which is placed centrally on the fabric, fold the fabric in half and then in half again. Crease the two folds and open out the fabric. Mark the central point, where both folds intersect, with a pin, and begin to stitch there, relating your stitching to the central point of the chart.

This method is satisfactory for small projects which can be worked in the hand. If the design is more complex, use a tapestry needle, and work a line of tacking stitches along the central folds (vertical and horizontal), using a thread which can be seen easily when the time comes to remove it.

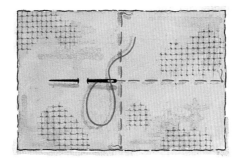

Preparing a Stitching Frame

The following method of dressing a frame is for both slate and roller frames. This preparation may seem rather laborious, but it is well worth the effort. It not only leaves both hands free to stitch in a stabbing motion, with the needle going straight up and down (the frame being supported on a stand or propped against the edge of a table), but it also helps with the tension of the stitches. Stitching with a consistent, even tension is the aim, and working on a frame certainly will help you to achieve this goal.

Make ½in turnings on the top and bottom edges of your fabric. Mark the centers of these edges. Machine stitch 1in/25mm wide tape to the other two edges.

Mark the center of the webbing on both rollers. With right sides together, matching the center points, pin the fabric and webbing together. Starting from the center and working out to the bound edge, stitch the fabric to the webbing using small, even overcasting stitches.

Roll the surplus fabric, if any, onto the roller. Slot in the side pieces of the frame; insert the pegs or tighten up the screws so that the fabric is held taut.

Using a large, sharp-pointed needle threaded with buttonhole twist or fine string, and leaving the thread on the ball or spool, so that you do not have to make joins, stitch through the tape on one side, lacing the fabric carefully to the side bar or batten with evenly spaced stitches.

Cut off the string or thread, leaving enough at each end to tie around the end of the batten. Repeat this process for the remaining side, tensioning the fabric as you proceed. Finally, tie off the ends of string or thread around the ends of the battens.

If your design is larger than the exposed area of fabric, you will have to undo this lacing before loosening the side battens and rolling the fabric on further to continue stitching. It is advisable to trap a clean sheet of tissue paper between the layers of finished work as you roll it on. This prevents any damage to the work itself.

Preparing the Threads

Stranded cotton has six strands which you will need to separate. Locate the end of the thread in the skein, and holding the skein at the band, pull gently on the thread until you have the required length. This should not be too long—a maximum of 18in is advisable—for constant friction as the thread passes through the fabric can result in a rather fluffy thread which mars the quality of the finished work.

You will now need to separate the strands of cotton, and the best way to do this is to take the ends of the cut lengths in the fingers and gently pull

them apart. Separate each strand and then reassemble the required number.

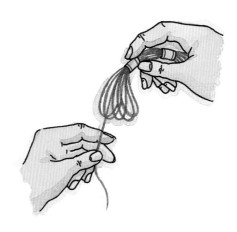

This will give a good coverage and ensure that they are not twisted around each other, which could cause problems.

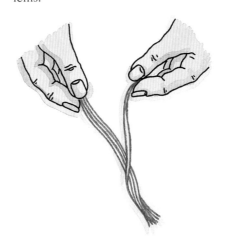

Threading the Needle

A needle threader is useful, but not essential, for finer needles. Pass the wire loop through the eye of the needle, place the thread through the loop and draw the loop back through the needle eye, taking the thread with it.

Otherwise, use the loop method. Loop the end of the thread around the needle and pull tightly. Slide the loop off the needle, nipping it tightly between your fingers, and push it

through the eye of the needle.

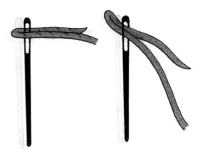

Threading the needle with metallic thread can be difficult. In this case, flatten the end of the thread by placing over it a small piece of paper folded in half, and push it carefully through the eye of the needle.

When working with blending filament, first cut and separate the strands of stranded cotton needed, place them alongside the filament which you have unrolled from the reel, and cut to length. Thread using a needle threader, or stagger the filament and strands, so that the filament goes through the eye of the needle ahead of the strands. Then, realign and use as a normal set of threads.

Alternatively, you could follow the manufacturer's recommendations and knot the filament with a slip knot through the eye of the needle to prevent it slipping.

Metallic threads are rather vulnerable, so, to prevent the friction that causes damage, it is advisable to work on a frame. Then the stitches can be worked in a straight up-and-down movement. It also helps to use a needle one size larger than you would normally use, which then stretches the holes between the blocks of the fabric, enabling the metallic thread to pass through more easily.

Cross-stitch Technique

Cross stitch has been used all over the world for centuries. It is a versatile stitch which has variations and can be used in numerous ways: for outlines, solid blocks of color, motifs and borders. However it is used, the same rule applies: the top diagonal stitch should always lie the same way.

The basic stitch consists of two stitches which run diagonally from corner to corner of a square, one stitch crossing the other. On Aida fabric the cross is worked over one block of the fabric; and on evenweave it is usually worked over 2 x 2 threads. It can be worked in two ways: by working individual stitches or by working a row of stitches in two stages.

Working an Individual Stitch

Bring the needle up at the bottom left-hand corner of the square, take it down at the top right. Cross this with a stitch which travels from bottom right to top left.

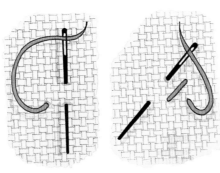

Alternatively, bring the needle up at the bottom right-hand corner, down at the top left-hand corner, and up at the lower left-hand corner. Take the needle down at the top right-hand corner and up again at the bottom left.

I prefer the first method because it mostly uses a clean hole (one not previously used). It is preferable to come up through a clean hole and go down through a "dirty" one so that the thread of the previous stitch is not split or snagged.

Working in Two Stages

Cross stitch worked in two stages takes slightly less thread, and is a quicker way of covering large areas. Begin by working all of the lower stitches in a row, and then return along the row, crossing these stitches diagonally. This method can be used horizontally or vertically.

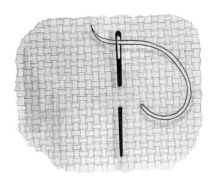

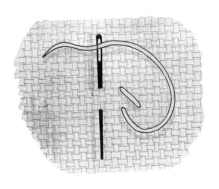

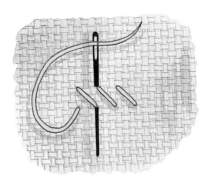

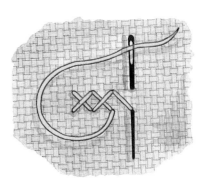

Starting and Finishing

When you start stitching, do not begin with a knot. This will make a bump which will show on the front of your work. Anchor the thread by making one or two tiny backstitches which will be covered by your first line of cross stitches.

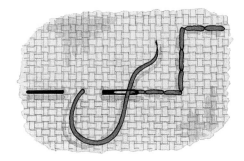

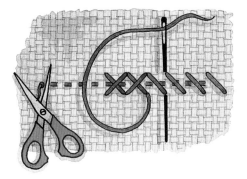

Alternatively, begin with a waste knot, as follows. Knot the end of the thread, and leaving the knot on the front of the work, insert your needle a few inches in front of the starting point. Work your first row of stitches over the thread which lies on the back of the work. Cut off the knot when the line of stitches reaches it.

When you have worked some of the design it is customary to start new threads by darning through the back of existing cross stitches. The same technique can be used for finishing off the ends of threads.

It is important, particularly if you are working with strong colors on a pale ground, not to carry threads across from one area of the design to another.

Stitches

Backstitch

Each backstitch is worked along one side of a square on Aida fabric, or diagonally across the square. On evenweave fabrics the stitch is usually worked across two threads of the fabric.

Beaded Half Cross Stitch

This is the simplest way to attach beads to the fabric. Thread a bead onto each diagonal stitch, making sure that all the beads and stitches lie in the same direction.

Hardanger or Kloster Blocks

Kloster blocks normally consist of five stitches worked over four fabric threads, although this proportion can vary.

Begin by anchoring the thread with a couple of backstitches, leaving an end to be darned in when the block is complete. Work five satin stitches over four fabric threads, starting at the bottom edge each time.

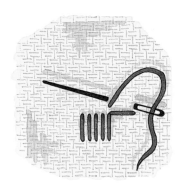

Bring the needle up at the bottom left corner to work the next block, which lies at right angles to the first.

Following the diagrams, continue stitching until you have four blocks arranged around a center square.

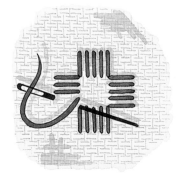

Darn the remaining thread under several kloster blocks; trim the end. Unpick the backstitches and darn in the beginning thread in the same way. When each unit is complete, cut away, with very sharp-pointed scissors, the small area of fabric in the center, taking care not to snip the satin stitch.

Slipstitch

This is a simple stitch used to finish hems or close openings.

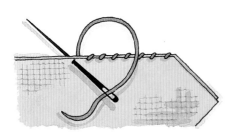

The two edges or layers to be joined are brought together with a line of small, diagonal stitches, which go through both edges or layers.

Ladder Stitch

This is a stitch which is used to close openings when the stitches must be virtually invisible.

Starting at one end of the opening, take a small stitch along the edge nearest to you, then take a second stitch

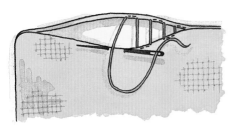

along the far edge, so that the second stitch starts opposite the end of the first stitch.

Work several stitches in this way, pulling up the thread as you work, so that the stitches disappear and you have a perfectly closed seam.

Four-sided Stitch

Each four-sided stitch is worked over a square composed of 2 x 2 blocks of Aida, working from right to left.

Bring the needle up at the lower right-hand corner, insert the needle two blocks up vertically, and bring it out two blocks to the left of the starting point. Insert the needle at the bottom right-hand corner and bring up at the top left.

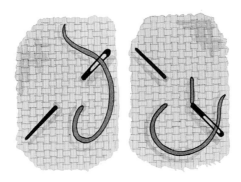

Insert the needle at the top right and bring up at the bottom left.

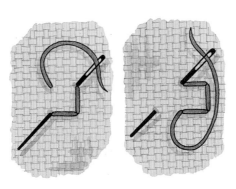

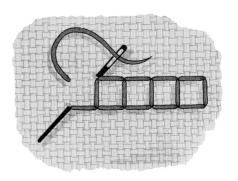

Repeat stages 1–3 to work a line of stitches.

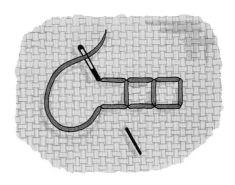

When turning a corner it is better to work in an counterclockwise direction. A neater corner is produced by turning down rather than up.

Finishing Techniques

Mounting and Framing

When you have put many hours of work into a piece of embroidery, it is worth taking it to a reputable framer for the final framing; however, you may consider mounting and stretching it yourself, using materials and method as follows:

Acid-free mount board. The thickness will relate to the size of your embroidery. Obviously the larger pieces will need stouter board. An alternative is foam board, a recent innovation, which is a sandwich of dense, polystyrene foam between two outer paper skins

Craft knife

Metal ruler

Cutting mat

Strong thread for lacing

Round-headed pins

Decide on the finished size of your piece and tack the outer edge of this shape in the correct position on the fabric. Mark out the board, slightly smaller than this measurement. Cut the board carefully, making several shallow cuts through the board rather than one deep one.

Place the embroidery face down on a clean surface. Place the board on top in the correct position, inside the tacked line. Starting at the center of the top edge, insert pins through the fabric into the edge of the board. Pull the fabric over the lower edge and pin as before.

Repeat on the side edges, pulling the fabric until it lies taut on the board. Use the tacked line to ensure that the grain (the direction of the weave) lies true, and does not wander.

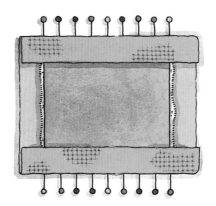

Using a long length of strong thread, work from the center out, lacing from side to side and leaving a length of thread free at the end. Complete the second half. Remove the pins on these two sides.

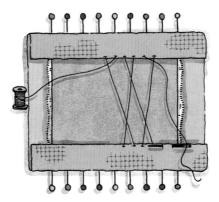

Starting from the center, pull each thread in turn to tighten up the lacing, and finally to finish fasten off securely at both ends.

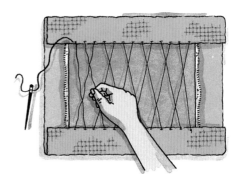

Lace the other two edges together in the same way, starting from the center and working out. Tighten up the lacing and remove the pins. It is not necessary to remove the original tacked line as it should be covered by the edge of the frame.

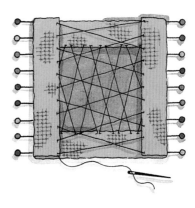

Covering a Window Mount

Covered window mounts are ideal for photographs, mirrors, even for cross-stitch pictures. The following instructions show just how easy it is to achieve a good result. You will need the following materials:

Acid-free mounting board

Craft knife

Metal rule

White glue or double-sided adhesive tape

Cutting mat

Round-headed pins

Cut the mounting board to correspond to the worked area of your embroidery, adding ½in to the vertical and horizontal measurements if you are planning to frame it.

Place the embroidery face down on a clean surface, positioning the mounting board on top of it.

Fold the outer edges of the fabric over the board and fix in place with pins. The turnover should not be more than half of the width of the board. Trim away any surplus and check positioning.

Fold the surplus fabric at the corners; crease and trim ½in outside the fold line.

Apply fabric glue or double-sided tape to the fabric turnover. Fold over

the corners and press flat. Fold over the short ends, then the long edges. Press flat and remove the pins.

Cut out the inside window, leaving a turnover measuring half the width of the mounting board all around. Clip into the corners, carefully, apply glue or double-sided tape to the fabric edges and press over onto the board.

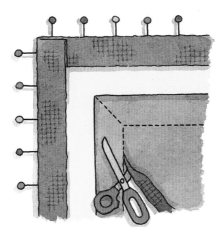

Mounting into Cards

Card mounts are the ideal way to display the smaller pieces of cross stitch, and to send those much appreciated personal greetings at special times of the year. The cards for mounting embroidery are readily available and easy to use, with a fold-over section to hold the fabric in position neatly. The

following instructions for mounting cross stitch onto cardboard apply to all sizes:

Card mounting board of a suitable size

Glue or double-sided adhesive tape

Iron-on non-woven interfacing (for larger pieces)

Small embroidered motifs need only pressing before mounting, but larger pieces can benefit from the addition of iron-on non-woven interfacing to the back of the embroidery, to give more substance.

Place the embroidery face up on a clean surface. Place the opened cardboard over it and check the positioning. You may need to trim the edges of the fabric at this stage if they project beyond the central window. Remove the cardboard, turn it over and run a line of glue or double-sided tape about ¼in outside and around the window, on the back.

Turn the cardboard over, and with

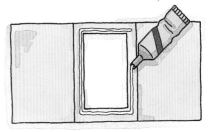

the front facing you, lower it onto the embroidery. Press into place.

Place the cardboard face down and run a line of glue or double-sided tape

123

around the four edges of the left-hand section.

Press this section over firmly onto the back of the embroidery, covering it completely.

Making Up a Cushion

All of the cushion projects in this book can be made up using the following tried-and-tested method. Piping cord adds a professional-looking finish, so also included are instructions for adding piping cord, making your own cord, and (for the more adventurous) making your own piping:

Cotton fabric, in a suitable color, the same size as the embroidered piece.

Machine thread

Dressmaker's pins

Tacking thread

Cushion pad (a cushion will always look better if the cover is slightly smaller than the pad.)

Tack stitch a square, which should be the finished size of the cushion, around the outside of the worked area, making sure that the center point of this square exactly matches the center of the worked design.

With right sides facing, pin the front and back together.

Machine or backstitch by hand along three sides of the cushion, and for 3in at each end of the fourth side.

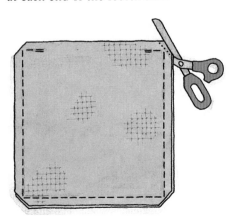

Miter the corners as shown, and trim the seam allowance to ¾in. Turn the cushion cover right sides out and insert the pad. Fold under and crease the seam allowance along the edges of the opening to give a stitching guide. Start at one end of the opening, closing it with ladder stitch (see page 121). Make sure that the small stitches are at right angles to the seam. Pull gently on the thread as you work to bring the two edges together.

Adding a Cord Trim

If you are going to add cord trim to your cushion, leave a gap of approximately 1½in in the seam when sewing up. Cut the cord about 2in longer than the distance around the cushion. Bind each end of the cord with machine cotton to prevent it from fraying.

Sew the cord on by hand, beginning at the opening, and tucking the starting end of the cord into this opening. Stitch in place by taking a small stitch through the cord and then a small stitch through the seam of the cushion.

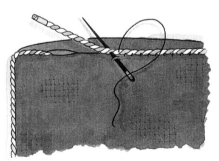

Continue in this way until the whole of the cord is stitched in place. Tuck the remaining end into the opening, laying it neatly alongside the first end. Sew the two ends in place, closing the opening at the same time.

Making a Twisted Cord

Instead of using a purchased cord, you might like to make your own, using one of the colors from your embroidery.

Measure the distance around your cushion, adding about 4in. Cut ten lengths of thread, each three times longer than this required length (for thicker cords add extra lengths). Put the lengths together carefully and knot as close to the ends as possible.

If you are working on your own, find a handy hook, knob or window catch over which you can slip one knotted end. (Remember that you have to be able to remove it later.) Thread a pen-

cil through the remaining end, and holding the pencil firmly and keeping the threads under tension, begin to twist, turning the pencil away from you in a clockwise direction.

Continue until the thread is very

tight and will not take any more twists. Keeping the tension taut, take hold of the center of the cord and bring the pencil to meet your first anchor point, the hook, etc. If you are making a very long cord you may need the assistance of another person at this stage.

Hold the ends together and let the threads twist back on themselves to evenly.

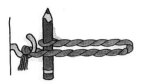

Remove the cord from the hook, remove the pencil and bind both knotted ends together with a short length of machine thread. Cut off the original

knots. You can now begin to attach the cord to your cushion, as described above, starting at the looped end—you will now have only one end to insert into the opening left in the seam.

Making and Attaching Piping

½yd fine cotton

Size 3 piping cord

Tacking thread

Machine thread

Dressmaker's pins

Cushion pad

To make the piping, lay the fabric on a flat surface and fold the top right-hand corner down to meet the bottom edge.

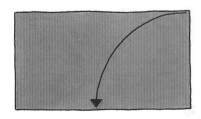

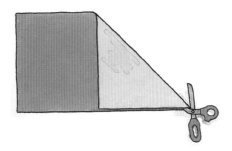

Cut along this fold, discarding the smaller piece of fabric.

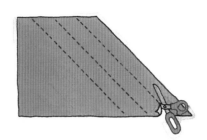

Cut bias strips 1½in wide from the larger piece of fabric, as shown.

Join the strips, right sides together, and trim the corners as shown, until the length is slightly longer than the measurement around the cushion.

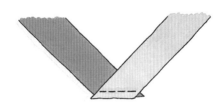

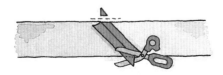

Make up a length of piping by folding this fabric strip in half, right sides out, around the cord and machining

close to the cord, using a piping foot. Leave a short length at each end unstitched.

Attach the piping to the cushion, starting in the middle of one side, by first pinning and then tacking again along the tacked line, forming the finished edge of the cushion. The finished edge of the piping should be on the inside, the raw edges lining up with the edge of the cushion. Clip the raw edges of the piping at the corners.

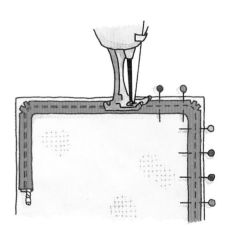

Join the ends of the fabric by making a small seam on the wrong side, checking as you do so that the completed length will lie neatly against the cushion. Cut away any surplus fabric from this seam. Two ends of piping cord will now project from the piping strip at this point. Neaten this cord by trimming so that the two ends overlap each other by ½in.

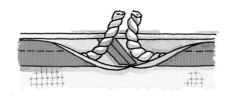

Separate the strands. Cut away some strands from each end, so that the total remainder makes up to the thickness of the original cord. Splice the remaining strands together as neatly as possible to make a continuous length.

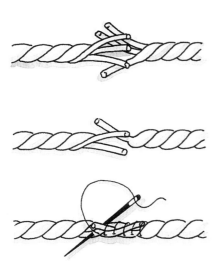

Anchor the join with one or two stitches through the cord. Fold the piping fabric over the join, and complete the stitching by hand. Tack in place. Machine the finished piping in place to prevent it from slipping when you assemble the cushion.

With right sides together, tack the cushion back to the cushion front, leaving an opening in the middle of one side which is big enough to insert the pad. Machine stitch this seam. Turn right sides out, and press gently under a cloth if necessary. Insert the pad and stitch up the opening using ladder stitch or slipstitch.

Making Tassels

1 Wind stranded cotton around the desired width of cardboard.

2 Run a matching thread under the wound threads at one edge of the cardboard. Pull up tightly and tie with a secure knot.

3 At the other end of the cardboard, carefully cut the wound threads and remove the cardboard.

4 Using matching thread, make a loop as shown in the diagram and bind the threads as tightly as possible, and knot the ends.

5 Trim the bottom of the tassel so that the threads are all the same length.

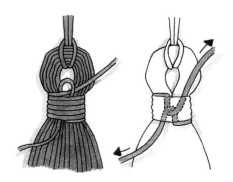

Cleaning and Pressing

If you have worked your embroidery in a frame, then all it will need on completion should be a light press, but if it has become soiled, wash it in cool water using mild soap or soap flakes, swishing the embroidery gently in the suds. Do not rub. Rinse thoroughly several times to remove all traces of soap. Do not wring to remove the water. Roll in a towel and squeeze gently to remove any surplus water, and press on the wrong side while still damp.

To press, place the embroidery face down on a soft, folded towel, and place a fine, dry cloth over it. Apply the iron gently, lifting and applying to each area in turn, and gradually working over the whole piece without dragging the iron across it. Repeat as often as is necessary until the work is smooth and completely dry.

Follow this method also for pressing dry embroidery, using a steam iron or damp cloth.

Threads

ANCHOR	MADEIRA	DMC
PROJECT		
PINCUSHIONS		
20	0513	498
46	0210	666
262	1602	3051
1044	1405	895
BACKGAMMON BOARD		
46	0210	666
246	1514	935
BOLSTER CUSHION		
231	1806	453
397	1901	3072
848	1708	927
847	1709	928
379	1912	407
376	1910	950
363	2301	3827
361	2013	738
375	2105	420
373	2102	3828
845	1607	732
843	1606	3012
393	1905	640
392	1906	642
BOUQUET TRAY		
35	0410	3705
46	0210	666
891	2208	676
1017	0809	316
1019	0810	315
873	0806	3740
972	0602	3803
76	0604	3731
859	1513	522
861	1602	520
862	1514	895
683	1705	500
877	1704	502
403	BLACK	310
BOW-TIE CUSHION		
400	1714	317
893	1814	225
895	1812	223
74	0606	3354
68	0604	3687
43	0513	815
234	1805	3072
323	0307	722
326	0311	720
47	0511	321
46	0210	666

ANCHOR	MADEIRA	DMC
CHESSBOARD		
01	WHITE	B5200
851	1706	924
1041	1809	844
403	BLACK	301
273	1811	3787
231	1806	453
274	1708	928
1037	1001	3756
SCHOOLHOUSE CUSHION		
128	1001	775
129	0909	809
131	0911	798
132	0912	797
134	0914	820
149	1006	311
323	0307	722
332	0206	608
1015	0407	3777
127	1009	823
CHRISTMAS DECORATIONS		
01	WHITE	B5200
245	1305	701
46	0210	666
FRUIT SHELF EDGING		
1007	2310	3772
11	0214	350
45	0514	902
210	1312	367
875	1702	503
879	1705	561
893	1814	225
1025	0407	347
1027	0812	3722
403	BLACK	310
313	2301	977
314	0201	741
842	1605	3364
844	1606	3012
846	1507	936
292	0111	3078
278	1610	3819
852	2205	3047
851	1706	924
860	1602	3363
854	2110	371
859	1513	522
1001	2302	976
330	0205	947
GLASSES CASE		
856	1607	3011
921	1711	931

ANCHOR	MADEIRA	DMC
1036	1005	3750
338	0310	356
1014	0401	3777
BOX		
01	WHITE	B5200
234	1709	762
235	1801	414
397	1901	3072
400	1714	413
403	BLACK	310
900	1805	648
1040	1813	3023
1041	1809	844
273	1811	3787
8581	1812	3022
399	1803	415
GARLAND CARD		
46	0210	666
20	0513	498
262	1602	3051
1044	1405	895
01	WHITE	B5200
300	0111	745
TREES CARD		
01	WHITE	B5200
403	BLACK	310
BELL-PULL		
01	WHITE	B5200
46	0210	666
943	2012	436
8581	1812	3022
401	1713	3799
MIRROR FRAME		
234	1709	762
01	WHITE	B5200
397	1901	3072
399	1803	415
235	1801	414
400	1714	413
403	BLACK	310
1040	1813	3023
8581	1812	3022
273	1811	3787
1041	1809	844
900	1805	648
IRIS HANDTOWEL		
879	1705	561
851	1706	924
119	0903	333
118	0902	340
142	0911	798

ANCHOR	MADEIRA	DMC
101	0713	550
IRIS SCREEN		
875	1702	503
876	1703	502
1042	1701	504
870	0807	3042
872	0806	3041
117	0901	341
118	0902	340
90	0709	3608
103	0710	3609
120	0901	3747
01	WHITE	B5200
LOG CABIN CUSHION		
46	0210	666
302	0114	742
244	1305	701
PLACEMAT & NAPKIN		
1007	2310	3772
11	0214	350
45	0514	902
210	1312	367
875	1702	503
879	1705	561
893	1814	225
1025	0407	347
1027	0812	3722
403	BLACK	310
SAMPLER		
46	0210	666
01	WHITE	B5200
401	1713	3799
8581	1812	3022
943	2012	436
STOOL		
246	1404	986
170	1005	3765
43	0513	816
19	0407	304
123	0904	791
204	1212	913
44	1514	815
832	2108	612
102	0714	550
148	1010	824
47	0511	321
895	1812	223
PASTEL LOG CABIN CUSHION		
46	0210	666
302	0114	742

ANCHOR	MADEIRA	DMC
244	1305	701
323	0307	722
25	0606	3326
206	1209	966
186	1201	993
161	1012	3760
131	0911	798
1016	0809	3727
398	1803	415
BOW-TIE TIE-BACK		
400	1714	317
893	1814	225
895	1812	223
74	0606	3354
68	0604	3687
43	0513	815
323	0307	722
326	0311	720
47	0511	321
46	0210	666
TREE OF LIFE CUSHION		
1210	—	121
1211	—	91
146	0911	798
143	0913	797
177	0905	792
ROSE GARLAND PICTURE		
1009	0306	948
868	2313	758
1013	2310	3778
1020	0501	225
1022	0404	760
1024	0406	3328
19	0407	304
897	0601	902
875	1702	503
877	1704	501
879	1705	561
403	BLACK	310

Index